# Praise for
# *In the Rapids*

"For those unfamiliar with what aboriginals have been saying, and where in broad terms they seek to go, *In the Rapids* represents a good first step to understanding."

*The Globe and Mail*

"A welcome statement .... In a poetic reference to the rapids in the title [Mercredi and Turpel] ask whether Canadians will continue to be tossed in the rocky rivers of inter-racial conflict, or whether we will choose some day to paddle a more peaceful river."

*Canadian Forum*

"Compelling ... offers insightful personal and factual perspectives on problems facing Canada's two million natives, and some thoughtful views on proposed solutions."

*The London Free Press*

"Thoughtful and thought-provoking ... a compelling case for redressing historic wrongs in the interests of building a stronger, more unified Canada...."

*The Vancouver Sun*

PENGUIN BOOKS

IN THE RAPIDS

Ovide Mercredi was elected National Chief of the Assembly of First Nations in June 1991. Originally from Grand Rapids, Manitoba, he currently lives in Ottawa.

Mary Ellen Turpel is an aboriginal rights advocate and an assistant professor of law at Dalhousie University. She lives in Prospect, Nova Scotia.

# In The Rapids

## Navigating the Future
## of First Nations

# OVIDE MERCREDI
## & MARY ELLEN TURPEL

Penguin Books

PENGUIN BOOKS
Published by the Penguin Group
Penguin Books Canada Ltd, 10 Alcorn Avenue,
Toronto, Ontario, Canada M4V 3B2
Penguin Books Ltd, 27 Wrights Lane, London W8 5TZ, England
Penguin Books USA Inc., 375 Hudson Street, New York, New York 10014, U.S.A.
Penguin Books Australia Ltd, Ringwood, Victoria, Australia
Penguin Books (NZ) Ltd, 182-190 Wairau Road,
Auckland 10, New Zealand

Penguin Books Ltd, Registered Offices:
Harmondsworth, Middlesex, England

First published in Viking by Penguin Books Canada Limited, 1993

Published in Penguin Books, 1994

1 3 5 7 9 10 8 6 4 2

Copyright © Ovide Mercredi and Mary Ellen Turpel, 1993

All rights reserved

Manufactured in Canada

**Canadian Cataloguing in Publication Data**
Mercredi, Ovide, 1946-
In the rapids: navigating the future of First Nations

ISBN 0-14-023345-8

1. Native peoples - Canada.* I. Turpel, Mary Ellen, 1963-
II. Title.

E78.C2M47 1994    971.00497    C94-931429-3

When I was with the Elders at Morley, a spiritual gathering place for our peoples, one of the Elders, Sandy Beardy, came to me and said he had a vision that all of us in Canada, including the First Nations, were entering a great rapids—a rapids no one has ever travelled before. No one knows the magic route to take. No one knows all the danger spots ahead, and there could be many. This is a journey I was told we must be part of. We must make the voyage together because we need each other. The Elder said our skills and knowledge will be needed in the turbulent waters ahead because we are experienced, having navigated many rapids in the past.

Ovide Mercredi

# Acknowledgements ☰

Many people have kindly assisted me with this book. At the Assembly of First Nations, I have enjoyed the help of Elsie Casaway, Harold Tarbell, and Karen Isaac. My appreciation is also extended to Bill Glaister for his advice on photographs. I am grateful to Jackie Kaiser of Penguin Books and freelance editor Greg Ioannou for their advice and support with editing the manuscript and for making it such an enjoyable learning process.

Particular thanks are owed to the University of Notre Dame Law School's Center for Human and Civil Rights which provided refuge for me as a visiting professor during the winter of 1993 so I could focus on this book and convalesce after the Charlottetown Accord experience. And a big thanks to Dalhousie Law School for giving me the latitude to do work for political change for First Nations peoples in Canada. Finally, thank you Ovide.

Mary Ellen Turpel
Prospect, Nova Scotia
June 1993

# Contents

# Entering a
## Great Rapids

This book is about painful experiences of the past and hopes for the future. It is about First Nations peoples, our experiences of history, our spirituality and politics and, especially, our relationships with Canada and Canadians.

The First Nations peoples, after being absent from the Canadian political scene for far too long, have moved into public prominence. The demise of the Meech Lake Accord, the Oka crisis, the tragedies at Big Cove Reserve and Davis Inlet, and the intense involvement of national Aboriginal leaders in recent constitutional reform discussions leading to the Charlottetown Accord have put First Nations peoples and leaders in the position of explaining to Canadians the profound challenges we experience and the solutions we favour.

While this new prominence is welcome—and certainly has made it easier to tell Canadians about the issues we face—it has not generally been accompanied by an appreciation of the complex historical connections that have led to the current situation, nor an understanding of the options available for meaningful long-term change. Information about First Nations peoples reaches most Canadians during crises and via non-Native media or politicians. The debate around the Charlottetown Accord showed most of us that much more work is needed to build bridges between First Nations peoples and other Canadians— and admittedly among First Nations peoples as well.

The Charlottetown Accord debate also revealed significant differences in how we interpret ideas of equality. Some Canadians believe that equality means everyone must be the same and that differences in lifestyle, culture, language and religion should be ignored if we are to share a democratic society. This is not an approach that First Nations peoples share because it means assimilation. Democracy must include respect for differences and the promotion of diversity if it is to reflect the realities of Canadian history. Some Canadians have inherited attitudes towards First Nations peoples and First Nations issues that we believe are not conducive to a healthy and vibrant relationship. Even the ideas of mainstream political parties often reflect outmoded assumptions about First Nations. This has to change. Genuine understanding must be fostered for the sake of more harmonious relations.

When we look at the national scene, five key areas stand out as sources of conflict between First Nations communities and Canadian governments.

First is the Indian Act, which has its roots in 1876 and is still in force today, governing the lives of Indian people. The Act has undermined the practice of self-government of all First Nations, and has caused great grief and injustice throughout its 117-year history. It has led to the rule over First Nations communities by a faceless bureaucracy so removed from Indian realities that it stumbles over its good intentions. In the manner of most bureaucracies, it tends to see Indian people as its property and is preoccupied with the control of that property. The Indian Act's arbitrary and discriminatory system for determining who is or is not an "Indian" has undermined First Nations identity with tragic consequences, threatening the very existence of our peoples.

Second, the Canadian government has not fully honoured or implemented the four hundred or so treaties and agreements entered into with First Nations. Some of these date from before Confederation, although numerous conflicts surround very recent treaties, such as the James Bay Northern Quebec Agreement of 1974. The repeated failure of the Crown to honour its obligation has broken the relationship of trust and now there is deep cynicism and disbelief in the sincerity of government among all First Nations peoples.

Third are the recurring disputes over lands and resources—disputes made all the more explosive by the massive dispossession of Indian land and an appeal process that simply does not work, even when wrongs are acknowledged.

Fourth are the tragic social costs of the attack on First Nations cultures and languages. Long-standing policies of assimilation and diminution of First Nations spirituality and values—through such vehicles as the residential school system—have undermined First Nations individuals and weakened communities. These experiences have resurfaced in First Nations communities in the form of alcoholism and substance abuse, family violence, depression and suicide. Skyrocketing rates of diabetes, heart disease, fetal alcohol syndrome and mental health disorders have created a health care crisis that is a by-product of the assimilation mentality that has insisted on changing First Nations lifestyles to suit southern Canada's industrial society. The social, health and economic problems of those living in urban areas are equally apparent.

Finally, we have the grinding poverty and economic destruction that have been mainstays of First Nations communities for the past fifty years. Subsistence economies that relied for centuries on hunting, trapping, fishing and gathering have in many cases been destroyed through a combination of development projects and unilateral restrictions on access to wildlife and resources. Housing standards and living conditions on reserves rival, and in some cases fall below, those seen in the Third World. When Bishop Desmond Tutu visited a reserve in Northern Ontario a few years ago, he was shocked to see conditions worse than those in the South African townships.

These five areas of concern, each of which is explored in this book, reveal a pattern of abuse, neglect and discrimination that has become our national tragedy. Some people have chosen to avert their eyes and close their hearts to the dramatic situation First Nations peoples experience. It is easy to do this when the problems are brought to the fore through a dry government report or another numbing news story. It is harder to ignore the problems when they are being described by those who know them from the inside. This perspective is the one we want desperately to share with you. We want all Canadians to know what the situation is from a First Nations person's point of view. Empathy and understanding is the way we want to build bridges.

After the demise of the Charlottetown Accord, many pundits and politicians repeated the practices of the past by confidently and paternalistically defining solutions on behalf of the First Nations. Some even suggested that the existing system is wholly adequate. Genuine First Nations approaches and perspectives must be at the heart of any Canadian initiative to address the problems identified above.

In some cases, Canadians who have recently voiced support for First Nations peoples have been motivated by the need to soothe a sense of guilt. They express regret for historic wrongs and revulsion for the current poverty. But guilt is not a solid foundation upon which to build better relations, although it may elicit greater reflection and understanding of the current situation. A quick-fix relief of guilt is not going to provide adequate long-term solutions. We would prefer to share experiences, create understandings, and expend the effort needed to build a better relationship. This will take longer and require more dedication, but it is the only path for genuine reconciliation.

This book is an attempt to bring to life the snapshot presented by national media when there is a crisis, a series of government discussions or another report on the dire problems First Nations peoples face in this country. While it offers a First Nations viewpoint, it is important to emphasize that First Nations views are divergent and no single work can embrace all of those various outlooks and ideas. It should also be noted that this book is about First Nations peoples; it is not about Inuit or Métis peoples, who can and will tell their own distinct stories. A note on terminology is in order here. The expression First Nations is used throughout the book because it captures how we see things: the first peoples who are organized in nations. The expression "nations" is not used in the sense of nation-states, but rather as distinct political and cultural communities. The expression "Indian," although not preferred, is sometimes used interchangeably in the text, as are the catch-alls "Aboriginal" and "indigenous," which are meant to embrace Indian, Inuit and Métis peoples.

Many fine books have been written recently on the First Peoples of Canada and of the Americas, particularly to coincide with the 500th anniversary of the so-called discovery of America by Christopher Columbus. Ronald Wright's Stolen Continents and Thomas Berger's A Long and Terrible Shadow are just two of the recent titles available. Regrettably, however, less has been written by contemporary survivors of Columbus's legacy. Much more sharing must occur if the problems we now face are to be addressed fully in a spirit of understanding and cooperation. This book is an expression of a commitment to the pivotal idea of solutions without violence.

Much of the education and debate that has been generated in recent years regarding First Nations peoples has come to Canadians through the words and works of Ovide Mercredi, the current National Chief of the Assembly of First Nations. In a sense, this is a continuation of an important political role forged by his predecessor, former National Chief Georges Erasmus, who raised consciousness of First Nations issues to a level that demanded the attention of media and governments. From that foundation, Ovide Mercredi has articulated the concerns of First Nations peoples tirelessly. His voice has truly been heard by Canadians, and his words have given First Nations peoples a sense of pride and acceptance, where there previously was little of either.

Ovide Mercredi is part of a tradition of many great Chiefs and spiritual leaders who have left an indelible mark on First Nations peoples and newcomers. These great past Chiefs, among them Membertou, Brant, Big Bear, Poundmaker, Manuel and many, many more, have shaped the image of First Nations in their respective generations and carried forward a message of how to foster the relationship with newcomers in keeping with traditional values. Ovide Mercredi is a Cree from Grand Rapids in central Manitoba. He has been National Chief of the First Nations since 1991 and before that the Vice-Chief of Manitoba. He is a lawyer and practised law in Manitoba. He has been an advocate of First Nations rights for more than twenty years.

Of course, Ovide Mercredi is not the only contemporary leader who has been actively bringing First Nations peoples' experiences to the eye of the public or government. Individuals like Inuit leaders Mary Simon and Rosemary Kuptana and Ron George of the Native Council of Canada also come to mind here for their efforts. There are many more whose words and whose vision for change do *not come to the public's attention because they make their voices heard in meetings, spiritual gatherings and other events away from the public eye.*

*But Ovide's views on non-violence and how we should approach those who oppose the rights of First Nations have been important to many of us because they offer a path for change that seeks to overcome anger, focusing instead on the creation of understanding among ourselves and with Canadians generally. My fear, as one individual, is that without a political commitment by Canada to the First Nations situation, anger and frustration will mount and the opportunities for non-violent solutions will diminish, while within First Nations communities suicide and social unrest will increase. In other words, the great rapids we are collectively facing will tip our canoes, and drown our hopes.*

*The next few years will be critical to Canadian history: they may be noted either for achieving acceptance or for rejecting First Nations peoples and rights. The strongest image I have of the decisive time we are passing through is of a medicine bundle that Ovide, along with the Elders, laid out on his Ottawa office floor. In the bundle were nearly all of the sacred medicines—sweetgrass, sage, tobacco and cedar—along with other items representing the many traditions of the spiritually diverse First Nations. As various Elders came to see him, they each added some new offering* to that bundle until office furniture had to be moved to accommodate it.

The bundle has been a metaphor for much of the First Nations message in the last while: we draw strength from traditional values yet place them in a contemporary context. Daily prayers for strength and discussions about strategy, justice and friendship took place with the Elders around that bundle. It is not less powerful because of its place in the Ottawa office; those values can infuse politics. In the same vein, First Nations peoples have a central place in this society and that place will not be determined by stereotypes of the "vanishing Indian" or presumptions that traditional values are tied to a bygone era of teepees and buffalo jumps. First Nations peoples' relations with Canada can and will be articulated in a contemporary context, but this will not mean the eradication of traditional values. These values—honesty, kindness, sharing and strength among them—are readily apparent no matter what issue is addressed, even though the context is wholly contemporary. From his views on civil disobedience to his ideas on how to fight poverty and substance abuse, Ovide Mercredi offers a powerful voice of change for First Nations peoples. His is a compelling plea for achievable social change that respects the rights and identities of the First Nations.

For First Nations peoples, history and spirituality are not written down in the sense of a book like the Bible—they are said to be written on the heart and passed along through story-telling, repetition and oratory. One thing most people realize almost instantly about First Nations leaders is that they are superb orators, especially when speaking in their own languages. These skills come naturally to First Nations peoples and we have many great speakers and leaders. In a reflection of the oral tradition—a tradition passed down as the backbone of First Nations knowledge, discourse and sincerity—many of the words in this book began as speeches. In this sense, the words in this book are not just the words of one man at one point in history, but the words of the many generations that have passed along the knowledge, ideas and values that have influenced and shaped his voice as one Cree person. In the interests of bringing forward ideas that might otherwise have only limited circulation, I ask the indulgence of the Great Spirit for the wilful break with oral tradition represented by collecting Ovide's oratory in written form. Readers may wish to note that the material in italics was written by me; the rest was written by Ovide, with the exception of this introduction, which I wrote, and the conclusion, which we co-authored.

*The authors' proceeds from the sale of this book will be donated to the First Nations Youth Healing Fund. Readers wishing to make contributions to the fund may send donations to: National Chief Ovide Mercredi at The*

Assembly of First Nations, 55 Murray Street 4th Floor, Ottawa, Ontario K1N 5M3 (613) 236-0673.

The book is an invitation to join us in making this country a leader in relations with First Nations and in the field of human rights. Along with many other Aboriginal people, Ovide and I continue to work for the recognition of the rights of the First Nations in Canada. The dream we all share is that some day we will be able to stop fighting battles with Canada over basic rights, and dedicate our energies to more peaceful paddling in regenerating communities.

Mary Ellen Turpel
Prospect, Nova Scotia
June 1993

# Turtle Island

*It is important for First Nations peoples to tell their stories— and most of those stories are about the past relationship between First Nations and European newcomers. For First Nations peoples, history defines the present; it is not something to set aside in pursuit of a better tomorrow. Stories about collective historical experiences reveal a relationship that is the basis of our current thinking about what did or could work in addressing the problems we face. This is especially true for First Nations with treaties dating from before Confederation.*

*Some people seem to think that the arrival of Europeans marks the dawn of North American history and that anything before this is pre-history and not terribly relevant. Some see the spread of immigrants as the destiny of history, choosing not to examine the consequences and continued costs of this view. For First Nations peoples,*

history keeps coming up and it probably always will because
the history of this country is the history of the original people.
You cannot understand Canada until you understand First
Nations experiences on this land.

The First Nations concern for history can be annoying
to some. In 1992, I facilitated several workshops at the
conference convened by the Government of Canada on First
Peoples and the Constitution, one of the five constitutional
conferences held for the elusive "ordinary Canadian." Many
of the non-Aboriginal participants in my workshop told me
that they were amazed at how much First Nations peoples
like to talk about history, and that they thought we did so
more than anyone they had ever met. While these non-
Aboriginal people's stories were about coming to Canada,
the First Nations participants spoke about the initial
encounters between the newcomers and their ancestors, and
about the sense of connection that comes from having always
been here in the land called Turtle Island. First Nations
peoples use the expression Turtle Island to refer to North
America, which is thought of as the shell of a turtle
surrounded by oceans. The images of the protective shell
jutting out and the living creature within make a powerful
metaphor for the connection with and respect for the land
that all First Nations cultures share.

The oral history related by Ovide below reflects the
mythology and experience of First Nations peoples,

*especially as they concern the encounters with newcomers. The kind of life the Cree people led before contact and the significance of that contact are both important in understanding how we find ourselves today: joined by history yet separated by culture and conflict.*

●●●

Events of the past decade and in particular the past few years have raised a number of questions among Canadians with regard to Aboriginal peoples. Throughout my travels, I am often asked such questions as: What do Indian people want? What do you mean by sovereignty? What is self-government? These are very real questions. Our own people ask questions of us, too: When did we become Canadians? How can they impose the Indian Act on us? When did we give up our sovereignty?

To address these questions we must know our history—a collective past that begins with the first European contact with our ancestors, although our history did not start with that event. The idea that we exist only within European history is a major misconception that is still taught. Columbus did not discover America; he was, in fact, discovered by the Taino people of the Caribbean. The "New World," as it was referred to, was populated by distinct peoples organized in diverse and culturally distinct nations. Each nation had its own defined territory, language, spiritual practices, economic institutions and political system. It was not vacant or empty. It was not new; it was ancient.

About five hundred years ago our ancestors met new people from other lands. It was a momentous event in our collective history, but we did exist before that time. Let me share with you how the First Nations have viewed our relationship with the land and explain how we envision the basis of a new relationship with Canada and First Nations aspirations for justice in Canada.

We have always been here on this land we call Turtle Island, on our homelands given to us by the Creator, and we have a responsibility to care for and live in harmony with all of her creations. We believe that the responsibility to care for this land was given to us by our Creator, the Great Spirit. It is a sacred obligation, which means the First people must care for all of Creation in fulfilling this responsibility. We have carried this responsibility since long before the immigrants came to our homelands.

The people of my origin, the Crees, lived close to the land as hunters and gatherers. The land provided, and still provides, food for our peoples, and we lived in extended family networks, travelling seasonally to hunt and staying at our favourite camps. Our life revolved around the four seasons and cycles of nature that the Great Spirit has given us. In the winter, we hunted large game; in the spring, geese and birds. In the summer, we harvested berries and fish. In the fall, we took more game and readied ourselves for the winter hunt.

Each of the seasons brought with it celebrations and reflections through ceremonies and social events. Especially in the summer when the weather was good, extended families gathered together to honour those who had passed on the year before, and participated in ceremonies like the Sundance and Ghostdance. We practised our spirituality or religion, which is in fact very simple: honour all living creation and maintain the balance of nature.

At summer social and spiritual gatherings, families chose mates and exchanged stories of hunting and the travels of the past winter; the modern version of these social events is probably the pow-wow. Before important events, men and women would fast and pray for direction from the Great Spirit. Prayer and reflection are important parts of traditional Cree life. It was important to be strong physically and spiritually, as it still is, and children were trained through puberty to assume their responsibilities by building their strength and endurance for adulthood. Fasting and participating in the sweatlodge were important ways to do this. Children learned about their place in the world through their mothers and with the guidance provided by the stories of the Elders.

We have faced our own holocaust here in this country. Many Canadians do not realize this, nor do they understand our struggle. This holocaust we have experienced has not necessarily been as a result of direct violence, although there was certainly some of that. The Beothuk people of Newfoundland are no longer with us—just one example of the price we have paid because of our contact with Europeans. We have also been diminished by sickness, the result of the lack of natural immunity to diseases introduced by the new-comers. More profoundly, we have suffered because of policies geared towards assimilating us and making us conform to the expectations of the dominant society that has been built around us.

We also cannot forget that many of our people died of starvation. Some of our greatest Chiefs watched their people starve due to the slaughter of the buffalo herds and expansion westward. Many tried, in despera-tion, to feed their families so they could survive, break-ing into Hudson's Bay Company posts to take food. Of course, they were severely punished for their acts to keep their people alive.

At the time of contact, Aboriginal peoples num-bered approximately seventeen million in North

America. Today our population here in Canada stands at approximately two million.

Because of this long holocaust, we now have to struggle to retain our cultures, rebuild our numbers and maintain our own distinct societies. While many of our ceremonies and spiritual practices have remained intact because of the tenacity of the Elders, our children do not always have the chance to learn how valuable these practices are because they are being educated in non-Native schools. People of my generation, my parents and even my grandparents know the pain of this experience. We went to residential schools—in my case in The Pas, Manitoba—where we learned nothing of our distinctiveness. We were just brown-skinned. We were often punished for being anything more than this, for example, if we spoke our own languages.

But you see, being Cree is not just having this skin—that is superficial. It is having a connection with the past, with the land. Our people have always lived here on Turtle Island. We always will. Our ancestors roamed the plains, hunted the woods, fished the waters that are now Canada. The spirits of our people are written on the land, our land. We cannot tell a story of somewhere else; we are this place. Our struggle is not about power or greed; it is about understanding and taking responsibility for the land.

Our history, told to us by our Elders and by our families, teaches us that to live a good life we must stay close to the land; we must share and respect the land and use that as a basis for our dealings with other peoples. It has been painful for us to deal with the newcomers and to learn of their rejection of our cultures and ways of life. Cree people have always been very egalitarian. Above all else, we believe in sharing and giving. This is a traditional value, and it is hard for us to believe that others would not be the same, but that has been our experience with European newcomers.

The struggle we face is difficult and few Canadians understand where we are and how we got here. We have lost so much along the way, yet by a miracle we have survived. Gone are many of our great philosophers. We have lost many of our teachers who were knowledgeable in the ways of our people and life on the land. We have lost traditional decision-makers and leaders who were expert in consensus and harmony. While we were in residential schools learning to be White, their knowledge was being ignored.

It has not been easy for us. Our experience with the European newcomers who created a political state called Canada in our homeland has left a bitter taste. So we need to talk about our grievances, because that is part of our history, too. At the time of Confederation more than 125 years ago, we had been so weakened and isolated as peoples that we had very little economic or military strength to ward off what was to come—namely, the further dispossession of our property, including our land and resources. We were seen as wards, as inferiors. But what was done to us, and what continues to be done, can never be justified. Canada has been built on this history and it has not yet faced its legacy.

We have never surrendered our right to be ourselves and we can never do so. This is a sacred responsibility. We have never abandoned our right to live on our land and draw from its resources in a respectful way. Our responsibility for the Earth continues. We must care for this land, our great Mother, because it holds our future and the future of Canada, too. We have never denied ourselves the basic freedom of all human societies, the one that derives from self-determination: the freedom to determine our destiny by the free will of our people. The first peoples of Canada had governments long before the European newcomers. Our peoples across the country had governments and unique ways of making decisions. For the Cree people, leaders were chosen because of their qualities of strength and responsibility. The Haida people on the West Coast were governed by a system of hereditary chiefs. On the East Coast, the Mikmaq people coordinated their government through a Grand Council, with "keptins" or Chiefs selected because of their political skill and spiritual knowledge.

We governed our people in a highly democratic way without using jails, formal courts or harsh methods of social control. Indeed, early European thinkers like Jean-Jacques Rousseau were impressed by the measure of liberty Indian people enjoyed here on Turtle Island. So we have long traditions in government. We are skilled in working together, co-existing with others on this land. Yet our self-government was denied us by the colonial and now Canadian governments. For almost one hundred and twenty years it has been denied to us by the Indian Act. That Act of Parliament may attempt to take away our freedom to decide, but we will never concede to such oppression.

We have been building ourselves up slowly in the past decades. We have seen what has happened and we will not sit by and acquiesce. Since 1969, we have made our voices heard nationally through the Assembly of First Nations and its predecessor, the National Indian Brotherhood. We have been rising to our feet to meet obstacles directly, to meet the challenges of life that face every one of us as First Nations citizens. But our history in Canada, in particular since Confederation, has been one of dominance—a dominance of Canada over us that has hurt our peoples in a very significant way. The pain is there at every level and the struggle against it is one of great magnitude. We have been reduced spiritually, culturally and politically. This has been unjust—we have done nothing wrong, except to be who we are, drawing upon our ancient history. This dominance in Canada continues to be the reality of our lives. Too often we define ourselves in relation to this dominance instead of in relation to who we are as peoples, and this will be an ongoing challenge. Our oppression by Canada has taken over our lives and we now must find ways to resist.

In 1864, the descendants of the people who arrived here five hundred years ago took it upon themselves to forge a constitution without us. It became the British North America Act of 1867. In this Act, the federal government gave itself the power over "Indians and lands reserved for the Indians." It did not ask us if we agreed; it just assumed power over our peoples. We were not even there when the decision was made. We must ask ourselves, "By what right did they get that power and how have they used it?" These questions are critical to our future relationships with this nation.

Has Canada used its power over us in the interest of our peoples, or in its own selfish interest? It has certainly not been used to support our peoples. The consequences of that kind of power are oppression and disregard for First Nations peoples' interests. The consequences are decisions in the best interests of someone living far away, in Ottawa or Toronto, rather than decisions in the best interests of First Nations peoples. The consequences are what we live with today: bureaucratic rule by the Department of Indian Affairs.

Our peoples used to identify ourselves. A basic right of peoples is self-identification. What happened to this process? Parliament decided it was up to them to decide who is and who is not an Indian. Canadian law now says there are seventeen different classifications of Indians. The Indian Act still makes distinctions between "Indians" and "persons." Sometimes we even argue among ourselves over which of the seventeen categories we fit into and rank ourselves that way. This thinking is oppressive. Now, tell me, how can we have seventeen government categories of "Indians"? We are many distinct First Nations. How could we have allowed this to happen? We have had no choice in the matter. There are no "Indians" except in the minds of bureaucrats. That term was Columbus's mistake, yet it has been our burden.

A people who are a nation define themselves. We know who we are. We don't have to wait for another people who have colonized us to tell us who we are, what we are and how we should live. But we have been colonized, not just in terms of government but in terms of our attitudes and minds. We are in a struggle internally to decolonize ourselves, to find out what it means to be a First Nations person. For me, I continue to learn what it means to be Cree because there is so much history to sort through, so much oppression to work out from under in order to find a personal balance. You see, it has not been just the government that has oppressed us. Our experience with organized religion and the church has also served to take away our voices. We were told for many generations that we were un-Christian, savage and godless heathens. Our ceremonies and beliefs have been attacked. As a child in Grand Rapids, I learned more about the Catholic church, where I worked as an altar boy and played the organ, than about Cree ways. I am even named for a Catholic priest.

It has been a spiritual journey for my identity as an adult that has brought me to know what being Cree means. I've had to work to learn that, because the schools, the churches and the government are all geared to making me erase that part of who I am, and who we are collectively. I cannot be fulfilled as a person without that knowledge of what it means to be Cree, and I believe this is the common experience of all First Nations peoples.

I do not condemn the church and Christianity; it is now part of our life, too. But it is not the whole story. I take counsel from Elders who are schooled in Cree and various First Nations traditions, as well as from those schooled in Christianity. We need to find wisdom in all places, to be open to learning about spirituality and how to live together. For me, the Cree ways are more important today than ever, for they will enable our children to have respect for who they are.

This is where we are as First Nations peoples at this moment in history. We have our own traditions and yet we've had this irreversible experience with the newcomers. We either continue with this dominance or we act as the free people we are and begin exercising our own self-determination and charting our own futures. We have to change our conditions for ourselves, our children, their children—and for Canada, too. The future generations will expect us to have answers and will want to know how we struggled for change. We must show them what we did to change our situation.

We know that the Indian Act was passed by Parliament to control our rights to mobility, particularly in Western Canada, so that we would not interfere with the westward settlement on our lands. Our people could not leave their reservations without a pass from an Indian Agent. That Indian Agent could say no; our

movement was entirely under his rule. This is the kind
of control we have lived under. Why should we uphold
that law and accept the right of other people to maintain a system of dominance over us? Why, indeed? We
must not be remembered as having accepted this treatment.

In Squamish territory, in beautiful British
Columbia, the potlatch was banned. The potlatch, like
the sweatlodge, was a very sophisticated and complex
system. It was a kind of government within a government. The potlatch was hosted by a Chief's family and
gifts were given to celebrate events or to forge alliances.
The family or clan blankets were worn and songs sung.
The potlatch is a highly symbolic and formal sharing of
identity and material wealth. It is all about extending
the circle of friendships and gratefulness. The gift is
important. The pleasure and honour of giving represents how highly our people value the principles of caring and responsibility. It instilled cultural values,
spiritual values and social values. Why was the potlatch
banned? Because it violated, in the opinion of some
missionaries and government officials, the values of the
dominant society. It offended the idea of maximizing
individual wealth or greed. The great sharing of the
potlatch was seen as pagan, ungodly, because too much
was given away. That system went underground for

many generations, but it has survived and is coming back. This shows how strong our drive is for the survival of our culture against all odds.

We have lived with this official Canadian denial of who we are and our ways of life. The Canadian state authorized the missionaries to stop the potlatch, and seized our gifts. And where are those gifts, including our sacred objects, today? They have been sold into the museums of the world to be displayed as part of the "lost" cultures of North American Indians. We have survived this insult to our beliefs, our spirituality, but we have scars. We have been impoverished culturally and economically by Canada's actions.

The newcomers and the missionaries always wanted us to conform to their view of the world, their idea of what is good. They wanted us to be like them, to assimilate into the dominant society, to relinquish our own values and accept the values they imported with them. They used every instrument to accomplish this, from forced education at residential schools to restrictions on our mobility. The Indian Act even made it illegal for our people to hire lawyers to protect our land rights or treaty rights. Until recently, we could not challenge the injustices done to our people in the courts. We could not vote anywhere until thirty years ago, and in the province of Quebec we only got the vote in 1969. The

Indian Act attempted to destroy many of the basic beliefs of our societies. It made our sacred Sundance illegal. It also made the Longhouse governments of our Iroquois relatives illegal, even though the Iroquois model of government was the inspiration for the American founding fathers.

After five hundred years, there is imbalance in our lives. After five hundred years, there has to be a reversal in positions, a harmony and a balance found. If oppression is our inheritance from Canada, what did we do to deserve this? How did we treat the newcomers from the beginning? When the Europeans arrived they had no land, no shelter; they were barely alive after their long voyages. They came as guests and we generously helped them. We gave them our food. We provided them with shelter. We taught them how to live here. We have always said we would share the land with them out of friendship.

Since the early contact with European people, our peoples have insisted that the relationship with the newcomers and settlers be one of equality. By this I mean the acceptance of the equality of peoples. Indeed, in the very early period of our relations, the European newcomers relied heavily on our goodwill and protection for their survival in an alien land with a harsh climate. The First Nations have always wanted the relationship with the Europeans to be based on agreements for peace and friendship, not exploitation or unilateral action. In fact, the early treaties were based on the concept of equality between distinct peoples with the goal of forging a more peaceful and respecting relationship. The fact that First Nations peoples were independent equals of the Europeans was recognized by the newcomers in many treaties, both with other European powers and with us. For example, the Treaty of Peace and Friendship of 1752 between the British and the Mikmaq was a treaty between equals; the relationship was based on a recognition that we are not subordinate to other governments.

Following the Treaty of Paris, when the British victory over France was declared, a Royal Proclamation was issued in 1763 to all British colonies, including Canada. It instructed colonial officials that "Indian nations" were not to be molested in their possession or enjoyment of their traditional territories, and that their lands were not to be taken without their agreement or consent. The Proclamation recognized that the First Nations were the rightful occupants of the territory now called Canada and instructed colonial officers to respect the rights of our peoples to govern ourselves without interference from the newcomers. This respect was not charity; it was required because we were recognized as distinct peoples living here before European settlement. That Proclamation is still the law in Canada.

However, our right to govern ourselves does not come from European proclamations or treaties; they just recognized what we were doing already. The Proclamation of 1763 did not create aboriginal land rights—it acknowledged them as pre-existing. We believe, as we are told by our Elders, that our peoples were placed on this land by the Creator, with a responsibility to care for and live in harmony with all her Creation. By living this way, we cared for the Earth, for our brothers and sisters in the animal world and for each other. Fulfilling these responsibilities meant we governed ourselves, and lived a certain way. This is the source of what we call our inherent right of self-government. It has a history that precedes the Charlottetown Accord by more than a millennium.

Five hundred years after contact our peoples have not been respected as we should have been by the newcomers. We "own" less than one percent of the land mass in this country even though originally it was all ours. That is how much life has changed for our peoples. Today we are told our rights are too costly. I find it absurd and ridiculous for some political leaders to suggest that the cost of self-government is too great, and that we should be forced to tax our people to raise revenue for improvements in our economic conditions. If they propose to give us back the lands and resources that have been stolen, these arguments make sense. But as long as they control our lands and resources, the suggestion that we should tax our people who are already poor is cruel and insensitive. How can you levy taxes on people who are unemployed at the rate of ninety percent in some of our communities? How can you raise revenues from the poorest people of Canada? The simple answer is that you cannot do it. You can do it only if the goal is to destroy us further.

Mahatma Gandhi was once asked, "What do you think of western civilization?" He replied, "I think it is a good idea." If someone asked me as a leader of the First Nations, "What do you think of Canada?" I would have to reply similarly that I think it is a good idea. But it is still incomplete.

Canada can only be completed through the inclusion of the First Nations in a new federal structure based on respect for our rights as peoples to determine our own futures. This departure is possible if representatives of the Canadian people commit themselves to ending the legacy of racism and colonialism against my people, to entering into a new relationship with the First Nations based on mutual respect, sharing and human dignity.

We want to participate in the restructuring of Canada because we bear this continuing responsibility for the land. Our identities and rights as distinct peoples flow from our relationship to the land, as do our Aboriginal title and our treaty rights.

We are the first nations of Canada and we will not allow the lie of only two founding nations—English and French—to continue. Canada is and always has been our homeland. This must finally be recognized. This lie of only two nations is particularly offensive to the First Nations because Canada's own history shows that our relations with the English and French were relations between distinct nations.

A continuity in treaty relationships, from the pre-Confederation period to the present, reinforces the fact that our relationship with the Crown is one of equals. Despite this reality, our relationship as equals is not respected and the promises made in the treaties have been consistently breached by Canada's governments. We have been dispossessed of our homelands even though prerogative instruments like the Royal Proclamation of 1763 confirmed our pre-existing rights and committed governments to dealing with us on a consensual basis.

In addition to these continuing injustices, we have also suffered at the hands of many racist and colonialist

policies devised by the federal and provincial governments. This has made it difficult for us to live our lives
with dignity in our own homelands. Although we have
had to endure these injustices, we are not the only ones
who have been affected by them. All Canadians have
been affected because they have inherited a way of seeing First Nations peoples that cannot work in a free and
democratic society.

Despite the Constitution Act of 1982, Canada's
constitutional values are still founded on the ideas that
were prominent in the colonial era—power, greed,
exclusivity and the rejection or denial of other cultures.
A great nation cannot emerge from these values.
However, there are other values that we have always
used to relate to all of Creation, such as respect, sharing
and harmony. These are also part of Canada's culture,
although they are not currently part of its political discourse. These are the values upon which First Nations
believe a new political order must be built. We are not
willing to passively accept totalitarian policies like the
Indian Act, and Canadians will not endure a political
future with many conflicts like Oka. No oppressive
regime continues forever, and we will struggle to end it
in this country. Just as former Prime Minister Brian
Mulroney applauded what people did to end domination
over their lives in the Soviet Union, the international

community is watching Canada and would applaud an end to its control over the lives of First Nations people.

The First Nations view our relationship today as a continuation of the treaty relationship of mutuality where neither side can act unilaterally without consultation. This partnership is symbolized by the grandfather of all treaties, the Iroquois Confederacy Gus-wen-tah or two-row wampum between your ancestors and those of the Iroquois. The two-row wampum committed us to a relationship of peaceful co-existence where the First Nations and Europeans would travel in parallel paths down the symbolic river in their own vessels. The two-row wampum, which signifies "One River, Two Vessels," committed the newcomers to travel in their vessel and not attempt to interfere with our voyage. The two vessels would travel down the river of life in parallel courses and would never interfere with each other. It was a co-living agreement. The two-row wampum captures the original values that governed our relationship—equality, respect, dignity and a sharing of the river we travel on. This is how the First Nations still understand our relationship with Canadians.

We want to work with Canada in order to generate respect and acceptance of our authority over our peoples and territories. We want to continue a dialogue

with you in the future so you will understand our vision
of a new Canada that includes us, and so that you can
be a partner in completing the circle of Confederation.
We must steer our own vessel. This is our sacred responsibility given to us by the Creator when we were put on
Turtle Island.

The First Nations will not beg Canada to recognize us as political entities when we believe international law already affords us that status. As peoples with
distinct cultures, languages, governments, territories
and populations in Canada, we must be recognized as
full and equal participants in the Canadian political
system. We can speak for ourselves and no one else has
the political or spiritual authority to speak for us.
Canadians cannot speak for us because Canadians are
different. To define us with Canadian heritage is to
enslave us. I call upon Canadians to deal with First
Nations as equals and end the legacy of dominance that
is as outdated as slavery.

# ≡ A Different Politics ≡

*Because most Canadians have had only limited exposure to First Nations peoples, few realize that First Nations leaders bring a different approach to politics than do non-Aboriginal politicians. Some people may have a notion of this, particularly if they have observed the political style of national figures like Elijah Harper and Georges Erasmus. But most have little sense of just how differently we approach the political process. In an era when all politicians are viewed with suspicion and some with ridicule, the assessment of a First Nations leader will ultimately be based on his or her fulfillment of the responsibility to treat others according to the traditional values of kindness, respect, sharing and compassion. While these values are clearly shared by Canadian society, they are definitely not emphasized to the same magnitude in Canadian politics.*

When I was a student of political science, most of the material I studied focused on scarcity of resources, competition, survival of the fittest and effective isolation of the opposition. Even the approach used by the instructors echoed these themes. These preoccupations are part of Canadian politics and it would be false to say that First Nations politics are immune to them. But these are not the main concerns or values of First Nations leaders. I do not believe First Nations politics are driven by these concerns. Our politics are premised on the will to sustain our languages, cultures and traditions. While First Nations leaders speak about what we have lost in the experience with Canada, the important point is what we are trying to preserve and revitalize.

People like Ovide Mercredi make it easier to be a First Nations person in Canada. His popularity makes our identities more acceptable and understandable to Canadians. His approach to politics is informed by the traditional values and spiritual teachings of Elders who are wise and knowledgeable about language, customs and traditions, and who can provide direction for others based on their own life experiences. The Elders are the most respected members of First Nations communities. They are both revered and feared for their insight and knowledge, and those who meet with them speak of feeling transparent in their presence. The Elders are able to sustain and promote traditional values *without having to blame, probe, cajole or give instructions to people. Their style encourages self-development and self-discovery instead of the application of a dogmatic set of rules that a person must adhere to, or else face discipline. If we were to try to find equivalents in Canadian society, we would say that an Elder is like a judge, religious leader, comedian and psychotherapist all rolled into one.*

*One of the marvellous benefits of working with Ovide Mercredi during his tenure as National Chief is the constant counsel of the Elders. Ovide works closely with Elders from many different First Nations: some have accepted Christianity, some practise their traditional religions, and others blend the two. He casts his net wide in order to get a lot of direction in decision-making and problem-solving. During the Charlottetown Accord negotiations, the Assembly of First Nations had a separate meeting room for the Elders, and whenever it was permitted, an Elder was present in the negotiation room to advise our delegation. Communal prayers and ceremonies were held every morning, and the Elders prayed continually that the participants would find a common understanding and accept aboriginal and treaty rights.*

*The importance of spiritual traditions to First Nations politics and decision-making cannot be over-emphasized. When bad feelings develop between First Nations leaders, one of them will organize a sweatlodge to enable those in conflict to come together and be cleansed. Somehow it's hard to imagine Kim Campbell, Jean Chretien and Audrey McLaughlin sweating out their differences with an Elder in a small shelter covered in animal hides. These leaders, to varying degrees, participate in a system that assumes that vocal disagreement and fervent debate will ultimately allow the best interests of the people to prevail.*

*First Nations peoples see it differently. First Nations cultures and identity are complex and no justice would be served by a thumbnail sketch. Cultures reflect regions, national identities (Cree, Ojibwa, Mohawk, Dene, Haida, etc.), and post-contact European influence and exchange. The diversity is vast. There are fifty-three Aboriginal languages in Canada, including Inuit and Métis languages. Only three— Cree, Ojibwa and Inuktitut—are said to have a strong hope of survival with a sufficient number of speakers and teachers to regenerate. Cultural diversity is also impressive. Ceremonies, customs and traditions vary across Indian country. But certain fundamental points are shared, like the central place of Mother Earth and honouring all of Creation.*

*Ovide Mercredi's spirituality, his ecumenical faith in the Elders to guide him, is an important part of his strength as a First Nations leader. He is not alone in this, as all of the powerful First Nations leaders share a common respect for the Elders and for their spiritual teachings, even though these teachings and values have been undermined in so many ways over the years. In January 1992, Ovide performed a ceremony with the Haida people at Old Massett on Haida Gwaii (the Queen Charlotte Islands) that demonstrates the profoundly spiritual nature of the movement for the recognition of First Nations rights and the healing of First Nations peoples. Be mindful as you read his description of it that this is a man who rose at dawn to climb a tree and tie a piece of cloth on a branch.*

●●●

Shortly after I was elected National Chief, I was asked to go to northern Saskatchewan to attend a ceremony that had been organized by four of the oldest Cree Elders in the Prince Albert Tribal Council. The Elders organized a sweatlodge ceremony where they blessed the headdress that they gave me and also explained to me what their expectations were of me as the National Chief. They gave me some guidance on how to conduct myself.

As part of some sweat ceremonies, those who participate present tobacco or cloth to the Elders, and when they make these presentations they also ask for some kind of guidance, assistance or prayer on behalf of themselves or others. On this particular occasion, the Cree Elders themselves brought the cloth, which we call prayer flags. They told me that during my term as

National Chief I was to find places to hang these flags,
that I should do this by tying a knot around a tree, and
that I should leave the cloth where I tied it. I then asked,
as anyone as unfamiliar as I was would, "Where am I to
hang these different flags?" They replied: "You will hang
the white flag here where the ceremony took place,
because the white flag represents the Creator and what
we conducted here was a spiritual ceremony." So I did
that. Then they said that it was up to me to decide where
to hang the remaining flags. So, after some reflection, I
concluded that I would hang one flag at the most wester-
ly community of First Nations peoples in Canada. Then I
would hang another flag at the most easterly location of
a First Nation in Canada. I would hang another flag at
the most northerly location of a First Nation in Canada
and then the final one, the fourth one, at the most
southerly location of a First Nation in Canada.

In the Cree, Ojibwa and Dakota ideas of the world
or the universe, what we call the cosmology, the four
directions are part of the unity of the universe and of
Creation. This is obviously important for me as a political leader of the First Nations in Canada. The flags
reflect the importance of our unity and our solidarity as
First Nations in Canada. They are a reminder, a symbol,
to all of us, not only of my duty to our peoples, but also
the duty of all the Chiefs and the responsibility of all

the citizens of First Nations to maintain a sense of purpose in keeping our people together for the common struggle. We must all share the need for unity if we are to ensure the survival of our people.

After the ceremony in northern Saskatchewan I asked the Elders to give me some more advice. I asked, "Which colour belongs in which direction?" And they said, "You will know which one to take at the time when you do it." I hung the green one on Haida Gwaii because of the beauty of the forest and the Haida people's commitment to the Earth.

*In his extensive travels across Canada to meet with First Nations peoples, Ovide Mercredi often visits Indian Friendship Centres. These places exist in most major urban centres so that Aboriginal peoples can gather, learn, find friends and feel secure in their identities in the face of what proves most often to be a pretty hostile urban environment. About sixty percent of First Nations peoples live in urban areas, off their reserves and away from their home communities, with especially large numbers in Toronto, Vancouver and Winnipeg. Some have moved away to find jobs or to attend school; others were not properly registered as Indians under the Indian Act and are thus prohibited from living on their reserves.*

If we try to deal with Canadian society in the context of power, political or otherwise, we will not achieve a better quality of life for our peoples, regardless of where they live. My hope is that if we can draw upon the wisdom of the old ways and our traditional values, we will have the strength we need to reach the prize we are seeking. Now, the old ways are the ways of the Elders: their wisdom, knowledge and kindness. The Elders teach us that these are most important because they lead to friendships and good relations and these things are what sustain us.

There is a harmony in the universe, among our relatives, among the animals and among all creatures. We are all relatives regardless of the colour of our skins. We, as peoples, should relate to each other in the spirit of harmony. And this is my understanding of the ultimate vision of our peoples: harmony and tolerance. We have a lot to contribute to peace in the world if we can be allowed to practise our cultures and traditions, if we can keep these philosophies alive for future generations.

To preserve our culture, and in particular these thoughts of the harmony between all living species in the world, we have to practise it. If our own conduct does not demonstrate a conviction based on these beliefs, if we do not use this guidance when we relate to each other, we will never realize the vision of our ancestors. This is a difficult task because we have been taught too well that we are inferior, our cultures primitive, our contributions irrelevant. We must stay true to the traditional teachings or we will never be able to share these things we value with the rest of humanity.

We must use our values to deal with the practical needs of our people—the need for better housing and education, improved health conditions, economic development and jobs, and especially the need to restore women to their rightful position of honour in our Nations.

These human needs are more important than anything else. At this point, how we try to meet them will determine our successes in reaching our peoples. When it comes down to it, these needs are no different from those of Canadian society in general. However, we do not believe in competition, in the survival of the fittest. We believe all should be cared for in our Nations, that caring and sharing, not self-interest, must be our overriding aims.

We have to appeal to what we hold in common with non-Native society. As the Elders instruct us with the acknowledgement that we are all relatives in this great Creation, we must reach out with more than anger or resentment. With this approach, I believe there is hope in Canada. But we must nurture this hope or it will evaporate. We can, as the First Nations, show the way of leadership, the way to create change, the way to create harmony in society if we maintain our values and our traditions and if we practise these ourselves in all our relations.

If we embrace our traditional values of respect, compassion, understanding and sharing and if we apply these values in our relations with each other, they will keep us united and will strengthen our peoples wherever they are. My mother, Louise, and my father, George, taught me these values and encouraged me to be proud of what I am: a Cree man. We are not inferior to anyone. This lesson we can never forget; we have a right to be different and being different does not mean being lesser human beings. Our values must take us forward so we can survive beyond this century. We must ensure, as we go into future challenges, that our peoples become stronger and stronger and stronger in the secure knowledge of their identities.

We will approach other people in Canada in the way our ancestors did, with generosity. But we will also resist continued exploitation and dominance. We have a rich heritage of nation-to-nation, treaty-to-treaty, government-to-government relations. By reclaiming our past, we will not destroy Canadian society, we will improve it. Justice for our communities, for all First

Nations, is justice for all of us. We know, based on our own teachings, that if you cause injury, if you cause harm, it will come full circle. Other Canadians have come to see that the hurt we experienced is a burden that needs to be removed. And we will deal with all Canadians in an honourable way. We will try not to be angry, although sometimes we are frustrated by the injustices. We will not seek to destroy relations. Our objective is not just to improve our society, not simply to reclaim our places as the First Nations of the territory now called Canada, but also to make Canada a much better country for everyone, and a model for the world.

*The Oka crisis erupted in 1990 after a standoff between Mohawks at the Kanestake Reserve outside Montreal and Quebec police over a proposed golf course expansion on lands claimed by the Mohawk people. After a police raid on the Mohawk community, barricades were erected and Mohawk Warriors stepped up their opposition to the expansion. The atmosphere intensified and the Premier of Quebec called in the army to police the confrontation. Sympathy barricades were established near Montreal at the Kanawake Reserve, and confrontations erupted throughout the summer between Mohawks and Quebecers who were inconvenienced by the barricade. Eventually both sides retreated and several*

*Mohawk Warriors were charged. Some have since been acquitted and some trials are still outstanding.*

*The Oka crisis had a profound effect on all First Nations peoples, as it did on Canadians and Quebecers. But progress towards resolving the underlying causes of the conflict has been minimal. Once the confrontation disappeared from national attention, there was little effort to build better relations between those who had been scarred by the process. Internally, the Mohawk people in Kanestake and Kanawake started to find ways to deal with the problems that surfaced during the crisis, but in terms of the larger relations with the municipalities or the province, or for that matter the federal government, the damage done has not been repaired. Indeed, in some cases the damage has been reinforced by other events.*

•••

During the summer of 1990 we in Canada saw events and scenes that, depending on one's personality or politics, either raised consciousness or triggered the most primary emotions. Whether or not you are for or against the Mohawk Nation, the Warriors, the Sûreté du Québec, the Canadian army, the Quebec government, the Department of Indian Affairs or its Minister, the federal government, Premier Bourassa or Brian Mulroney, one thing is certain: none of us can escape the impact, the implications or the consequences of the imbalance in the relationship between Canada and the First Nations. We must live with what we saw in the show of force against Mohawk people.

As a result of the conflict at Oka all of us have come to at least one realization—that ignoring the rights and aspirations of the First Nations in this country will imperil the unity and stability of Canada. There can be only one logical conclusion: in the interest of peace, justice and respect for First Nations peoples and their collective rights and freedoms, the people of Canada must insist that their governments take immediate measures that will promote an end to this pattern of dominance and oppression. The adversarial approach demonstrated by the federal and provincial governments must give way to a new form of inter-action based on a policy of respect, dialogue and co-operation.

In every crisis there are at least a thousand lessons to be learned and therefore at least a thousand opportunities. The crisis facing our country at Oka showed all of us the value and importance of human respect, kindness and justice—the value of drawing upon these virtues before relations break down, because breakdowns are likely. This approach to preventing conflict in human affairs requires the reparation of wrongs and injustices before they are repeated. We are ready for this. We must all work together to help our respective governments succeed in making genuine reparation a reality.

But first we have to understand our current situation. We know that relations between our peoples and Canada have been damaged due, in no small measure, to the contempt for peace and justice that was dramatically displayed by the acts of omission and commission perpetrated by the federal government. By refusing to participate in negotiations to resolve the conflict at Kanestake and Kanawake, the federal government neglected its responsibilities towards Mohawk people, and by this act of omission contributed to the needless escalation of that conflict.

By sending in the army at the request of Premier Bourassa, the federal government brought into play a new level of racial contempt and raised the level of racial intolerance and mistrust in Canada. Unfortunately, this may result in a deep and long-lasting negative effect on the future treatment of Aboriginal people by the dominant society, with a corresponding deterioration of Canada-First Nations relations in Quebec. At a time in our history as Aboriginal peoples when we are concentrating on healing our communities and focusing on recovery, we can ill afford the time or energy to fight the Canadian government or, for that matter, the rearguard racism that surfaced at Oka.

At this moment in our common destiny, my people are grieving again. It seems that each time we begin to move towards an accommodation based on mutual respect, the national government responds by either doing something negative or doing nothing when required to act positively, thus nullifying all the hard-earned goodwill and understanding. We cannot afford governments that spoil these opportunities for real change. Aboriginal peoples should be able to celebrate success, victories and progress, too. We should not be placed in a position where we are always grieving due to one injustice after another. We have a right to be happy, too, and to live a better life in Canada. But there is not much room for happiness in our common interaction, past or present.

For us, Oka symbolizes a continuation of a classic historical precedent in human relations that we all must work to change. Dominance as practised by one member of the human family in the name of rightful dominion over another distinct member of the human family is as outdated as the idea that the world is flat. Words and phrases such as "one law for all," "we are all Canadians," "the rule of law" or "law and order" will remain shallow and hollow rationalizations until such future time in our common destiny when Canadians and their governments decide to accept and respect our human right to remain and grow as distinct members of the human family.

No matter how hard one may try to legitimize the supremacy of Canadian society, one cannot deny that the consequences of that supremacy include the denial of Aboriginal self-determination and the entrenchment of bondage. We find no happiness in that relationship. Our Elders tell us that it is good for our soul to grieve this kind of imbalance in our relationships. Grieving reinforces our belief that we should strive for balance and harmony in our lives and to treat each other with dignity and respect at all times. Grieving, we are told, is an essential part of the healing process. It leads to recovery. It results in peace and harmony, in wholeness with all life. For our country to heal, all Canadians need to express sorrow for the loss of our rights and freedoms. Indeed, with that kind of support and strength for Aboriginal peoples and our collective rights, we all help to accelerate the new dawn of understanding between different peoples in Canada.

This healing process needs to be applied with the same conviction and honesty in our relations with Quebec. There is still time for all of us to arrive together at a place of mutual celebration and happiness. It would be in our collective interest, as peoples sharing the same soil of Mother Earth, to find a common reason to celebrate in peace and respect.

Mahatma Gandhi had a profound influence on me as youngster growing up in a remote community in Manitoba. I encountered Gandhi when I was very young. Before anyone concludes that I have either a vivid imagination or no respect for the truth, let me provide more facts. I don't recall my age when I first learned of this man, Gandhi, but I do remember I had already started school and I was already able to read enough English to understand the written English in books and magazines. I am guessing that I was at least eight years old. A few of us Cree children were visiting a Catholic priest in my home village of Grand Rapids, Manitoba, when I came across a copy of *Life* magazine that carried the story of the life and death of the great spiritual leader Gandhi.

I still remember seeing the grief on the faces of thousands and thousands of people mourning his death. It occurred to me that burning the body was quite a different practice from the rite of death I knew. Cree people are buried, not burned, when they die, and I was surprised at how Gandhi was treated. More than this, I was surprised to see that Gandhi's people didn't dress

like anybody else I had ever known. Since then, my village has expanded and I have seen many things that are
different from Cree ways.

I was not a good reader in those days. I remember
more from the pictures of that *Life* magazine than I do
of the written stories that accompanied them. It
occurred to me that this was no ordinary man—that he
had been deeply spiritual, that the people loved him
immensely, that he had been involved in some great
deeds in the interests of peace, and that his death was in
fact a loss to all of humanity. I felt that loss. I was sad.
But at the priest's house in Grand Rapids, I was just as
certain that he was in heaven.

Since my youth, I have become a reader of some of
the writings and several of the books by or about
Gandhi. Although far from being a scholar or even a
serious student, I do know his teachings as they may be
applied or adapted to our political resistance to end the
injustice and oppression of the First Nations in Canada.
The concepts of passive resistance, non-violence, truth
force and civil disobedience significantly shaped my
approach to politics, although they have been overshad-
owed somewhat in recent years by the more spiritual
teachings of this extraordinary human being. As one
gets older, one's interests change. This is not to suggest
that the political principles and practices of Mahatma

Gandhi have no relevance to the First Nations or to Canada. We could certainly have benefited from Gandhi's moral authority, had he been around to apply his teachings and philosophy of conflict resolution inside the cabinet rooms in Quebec and on Parliament Hill as well as in the Councils of the Mohawk Warrior Society.

Gandhi's philosophy of non-violent resistance as a means for changing society is not for the weak of mind, the greedy or the cowardly. Non-violence and civil disobedience in the face of brute force, oppressive neglect and governmental tyranny require discipline, conviction, courage and sacrifice. It is far easier to succumb to anger and resentment and to resort to violence than it is to be generous and kind to your oppressor. Unlike violence, "*ahimsa*" or the way of non-violence is a discipline. Violence is a negative force, while *ahimsa* is a positive force.

In Gandhi's own words we can see that his philosophy is a way of life, not just the means for carrying out political action:

> Non-violence is a power which can be wielded equally by all children, young men and women or grown up people—provided they have a living faith in the God of love and have therefore equal love for all mankind. When non-violence is accepted as the law of life, it must pervade the whole being and not be applied to isolated acts.*

*All Men Are Brothers, Words of Mahatma Gandhi, compiled and edited by Krishna Kripalani, (UNESCO, 1958, 4th edition) p. 91.

Within our indigenous societies, we also have many teachers who show the superiority of the path of non-violence. Our spiritual Elders teach us that love and compassion are the substance of human respect and understanding. We are taught the concept of non-co-operation with evil or with harm, whether active or potential. Non-cooperation is a response. It does not mean burying your head in the sand, hoping that the problem will go away by itself. Resistance can be passive or active but by not cooperating with negative forces you give them no opportunity to go anywhere but away from you. We learn to repel force not with less, equal or more force, but with non-cooperation.

In our traditional teachings we are told we have a choice. You can always walk away from conflict or you can walk into it. If you are so inclined, you can create conflict, but you can also defuse it. This means you can be a troublemaker or a peacemaker. The choice is yours. In the end, what occurs is what you have decided to do or not to do.

Human problems exist to be solved. In most cases such solutions are within our immediate grasp or control. In certain situations, we need assistance. In all cases we need "shakeetowin," which is Cree for love, and "keesaywatisseewin," which is Cree for kindness or compassion. We have ceremonies, spiritual practices

and prayers to help us resolve conflict by restoring balance and harmony. At Kanestake, the anger and the
hatred felt by the Warriors was replaced by feelings and
thoughts of peace and harmony, not because the
Minister of Indian Affairs, Tom Siddon, called for
respect for the rule of law, but as a direct result of the
role of traditional First Nations spirituality. The peace
pipe, ceremonies, drums, songs and prayers of Mohawk
Elders and spiritual leaders from the Iroquois
Confederacy helped to defuse that conflict.

As you can see, non-violence in human relations is
also a teaching of our traditional spirituality. When
practised, it becomes a way of life and a positive life
force. Like Gandhi, our political leaders can also apply
these traditional teachings to our political action. We
do not have to resort to violence as a means to an end.
Civil disobedience, in its purest form as advocated by
Gandhi, does not result in violence.

Our Elders remind us that we all have a rich heritage and tradition of peaceful co-existence in Canada.
All we need to do is apply the teachings of harmony
into our daily lives and in our collective actions. It is
our duty to our ancestors to maintain these traditions
for the benefit of present and future generations of our
people. These are complex issues and choices.
Aboriginal peoples reject the path to violence for many

reasons. First and foremost, it is contrary to our traditions and the teachings of our Elders. Second, in a
racially mixed society such violence leads to greater
racial strife because of reactionary racism. Third, violence is a negative force that leads to self-destruction
and more aggression. Fourth, in Canada the potential
for violent retaliation from the adversary is far greater
than can be imagined. Fifth, violence breeds violence.
Sixth, violence destroys people and potential relations.
Finally, there is no honour in violence.

We will continue, as our ancestors taught us, the
path of non-violence. It is a positive force. As such, this
path leads the way to resisting injustices without
destroying ourselves or, for that matter, our opponents
or adversaries. This is also the path for recovery. Non-
violence at home, at work, in the community and in our
dealings with all people will help us in strengthening
our people and First Nations. Non-violence frees us
from the negative energy of a violent confrontation; its
positive force allows us to concentrate our energies in
the recovery and enrichment of our peoples and distinct
nations.

# $=$ **Mending Broken** $=$
# **Treaty Promises**

Almost since the initial contact between Europeans and the First Nations, we have been negotiating treaties. The treaties are a connecting thread through the history of the relations between the first peoples and the newcomers. As early as the 17th century in what is now known as Eastern Canada, First Nations entered into treaties with Europeans of Dutch, French and English extraction. These treaties represent relationships between distinct peoples or nations reached after discussion and negotiation. Indeed, the treaty negotiation and ratification ceremony reflected First Nations culture and tradition more than European approaches. A pipe ceremony accompanied the agreement to symbolize the sacredness of the commitments. The First Nations treaties are like the treaties between sovereign nations that are entered into today. To draw on a contemporary example, the North American Free Trade Agreement is a treaty among

three nations—Canada, the United States and Mexico.
First Nations treaties, particularly the early treaties from
before Confederation, were treaties of peace and alliance
that sought either to keep the First Nations neutral or to
garner their support in inter-European battles, such as the
French-English wars, the United States Civil War and the
War of 1812. In exchange for military friendship or
alliances, the First Nations were given express recognition of
their rights of hunting and trade, and were promised that
they would not be disturbed in their enjoyment of their lands.
Goods were pledged annually by the Crown to the First
Nations to fulfill and renew the treaty commitment and in
many cases these are still given on the anniversary of the
treaty signing.

Probably the best example of these early agreements are
the Maritime treaties of 1726–1781 between the British and
the Mikmaq. These treaties are still in force today—the
Supreme Court of Canada made this clear during the 1980s
in a landmark decision to uphold the hunting rights
guaranteed the Mikmaq in the Treaty of 1752. While two-
hundred-year-old treaties may seem irrelevant, they are in
fact very relevant to Canadians as well as First Nations
peoples.

The history of Canada is different from the history of
the United States in its dealing with Indian tribes. In
Canada, instead of fighting battles, the British Crown made

alliances with First Nations through treaties negotiated by agents or officials of the Crown. This was a pragmatic policy: for the most part, attacks would not have been successful, because of the small, scattered settlements in Canada and the military superiority of First Nations warriors. In Canada, First Nations were not "conquered" in some military sense. A relationship evolved, and it has been remarkably peaceful, particularly in contrast with Aboriginal-newcomer experiences elsewhere in the world. The treaties have been an important part of this peaceful relationship. Some, like Treaty Number Six in Manitoba, Saskatchewan and Alberta, provide that the Chiefs will maintain peace among their people and in the dealings their people have with others. During the Oka crisis some Chiefs advocated peaceful resolution of the conflict at Kanestake because they considered confrontation to be a breach of their treaty promise to maintain peaceful relations between their people and Canadians.

The treaties are also critical to Canada's history because, at least in most of Central and Western Canada, the treaties are the basis for the Crown's claim to lands. Not all treaties deal with lands, but those that do contain specific provisions stipulating that Indian land interests were ended in exchange for other promises. These texts do not accord with First Nations interpretations of the treaty negotiations. First Nations see the treaties as calling for a sharing of land in *exchange for promises made to First Nations about their continued land rights and the recognition of their customs and their autonomy. The treaties which deal with land transfers have little in common with real-estate transactions from a First Nations perspective. Our Elders teach us that the treaties did not extinguish Indian title. Where no treaties exist, it is difficult to pinpoint legally whether Canadians have acquired clear rights to lands that they settled when these were already occupied and owned by someone else. We now have land claims because in some parts of Canada there were no treaties and no battles, so the legal basis for the Crown's ownership of lands is dubious. The idea that North America was vacant and thus settlers could come and take all they wanted is obviously untrue. First Nations have occupied different regions of Canada since time immemorial. Two hundred years is just a little blip in the history of this land, even if it seems like an unimaginably long time ago to those who have descended from European settlers.*

*The goal of the treaties was to allow for settlement and to gain the friendship and alliance of First Nations, but the Crown agents who negotiated them did not always act in good faith. The First Nations were given assurances during negotiations only to later find out that the written text did not reflect these promises. Of course, there were serious problems of translation. First Nations peoples had no concept of individual ownership of land, so the idea*

that land could be ceded by a treaty was a shocking and
alien concept. Misunderstandings over the terms of the
treaties have caused grievances almost since the moment
they were signed.

Especially in this century, the Crown has acted in a
seemingly willful manner to undermine the treaties. Even
though the treaties were the product of negotiations and
consent, the governments of Canada have passed legislation
and acted in ways that are contrary to their treaty obligations,
without even consulting us. This has led to serious unrest and
injustice. It has also caused First Nations to lose respect for
Canada as a nation because governments are seen as
unwilling to keep their word and honour their solemn
commitments. In fact, during the repatriation of the
Constitution from the British Parliament to Canada in 1981,
First Nations from Alberta, joined later by others, argued
before the British courts that it was illegal for the Queen to
transfer the obligations to the Canadian government for the
treaties when these were entered into with the British
Monarch. The British courts did not accept this argument,
but they did state that all the obligations in the treaties that
were passed to Canada from Britain had to be honoured and
were constitutional obligations on the Canadian government.

It has been an important political goal for First Nations
to have treaty grievances addressed by the Canadian
government, but the government has given little indication

*that it is open to discussion. How to go about resolving treaty grievances is a matter that is still being debated within First Nations political circles. Many First Nations peoples believe that any process that would compromise the nation-to-nation nature of those agreements would be unacceptable, and want to deal only with the federal Crown, since it was the original signatory for the government at treaty time. This would mean no involvement by provincial governments. Other First Nations see a pragmatic need to involve provincial governments as extensions of the Crown, given that provincial governments have control over lands in Canada. In some rare instances, First Nations still want the British Crown to deal with their treaties. The ongoing internal debate is complex but commitment to the treaties is unequivocal.*

*During the Charlottetown Accord referendum debate, some treaty First Nations refused to discuss or support the Accord proposals because they believed that any agreement for constitutional reform reached with the provinces would diminish the stature of their treaties. This position reflects the fact that at treaty time, those bands were dealing only with the federal Crown. This was a significant factor in the First Nations debate, although it was perhaps based largely on fear; the proposals gave each treaty First Nation the choice of whether or not to include provinces in their treaty implementation discussions. Nevertheless, this reluctance can be understood by looking at the broader context. Many of the treaties date from an era when provinces were not powerful forces. In some cases the provinces did not even exist. This was either pre-Confederation or before the entrance of key provinces into the young federation. Hence, the oral history of the treaties developed when Canada was a fairly centralized state, and it does not fit well with the current political reality that Canada is now one of the most decentralized federations in the world. Provinces have enormous political power and it is difficult to see a way of addressing grievances without provincial government compliance with the terms of the treaties. The Canadian state has changed fundamentally over the years and responsibility for fulfilling the treaty obligations no longer rests solely where it did two hundred years ago.*

Some questions have arisen as to whether the treaty process was one-sided. We must remember that while the treaties were written in English or French and were based on foreign legal concepts, we also have an understanding of these treaties, a knowledge of these treaties that is no less the truth and no less valid simply because it is oral. Disagreements on what the treaties mean and how they should be implemented are not an excuse for Canada to avoid fulfilling its treaty obligations. It is a duty of the Canadian government to sit with our people and to reach a consensus on what the terms of the treaties mean and how they should be implemented. From our perspective, nothing has changed; the only thing that is new is Canada's reluctance to respect the treaties of the past. The First Nations view treaties as sacred. They are to endure for as long as the sun shines and the rivers flow. They cannot be destroyed, ignored or forgotten. They cannot be wished away.

The treaties are not responsible for our problems today. They have not converted our people into inferior human beings. The relationship of dominance we have experienced is a product of government policies like the Indian Act, not a product of the treaties. Our freedom, our liberation, will not be secured simply by looking at legislative changes. Why should we beg another nation to modify its laws so that it will not violate our rights? Our rights were negotiated and secured by our ancestors; we must look beyond the laws passed by Parliament and the provinces and find other ways of guaranteeing protection for our treaties and treaty rights. Before 1982 the courts of this land interpreted our treaties as inferior documents, capable of being changed at whim without our consent by provincial and federal politicians. This happened even though our treaty rights were in many cases explicit. No one can say there is any ambiguity about the nature or scope of these rights to hunt, fish, trap and gather food. Yet we saw the federal government diminish the treaties by enacting fisheries and wildlife laws. They were not blind to the commitments they had made to our forebears; they just chose to disregard them.

The limits on our treaties did not result from decisions made by First Nations peoples or organizations. No First Nations person consented to any of these measures. No First Nations person has broken ranks to agree to diminish or alter treaty rights. Let us remember that all the efforts to undermine treaties and treaty rights have been on the part of the other side, the Crown. We respect the rights of First Nations to deal directly with the federal Crown as nations respecting those treaties; we have never deviated from that principle and we never will. Yet we know that federal government legislation has nearly succeeded in reducing the treaties according to its whims. We must reverse this and the question is, how do we do it? We have diverse opinions on treaties so we must find a way to make changes that accommodate the different approaches of our peoples. In some parts of our country, people do not want the terms of their treaties discussed further; they just want them honoured. In other parts of our country, our peoples believe that their treaties are fraudulent agreements; they want them renegotiated because the text does not accord with their understandings. In still other parts of the country, our First Nations want a bilateral process to clarify the meaning of terms of the treaties in a contemporary context.

When it comes to the involvement of the provinces, we must debate this issue. Some First Nations want to proceed on discussions with provinces without undermining the discretion of other First Nations who want to deal only with the federal government. In some regions, the provinces were involved in negotiating treaties and they cannot now be ignored when they have responsibilities to implement their obligations; the Province of Ontario is an example. We also have modern-day examples of treaties like the James Bay Northern Quebec Agreement, which included the involvement of the Province of Quebec.

So we are trying to find answers that will accomplish our common objective yet allow flexibility for different treaty First Nations needs. The common objective that we all share regarding treaties is that we want our treaty rights to be fully enjoyed by our peoples. We have witnessed more than two hundred years of neglected treaty promises in Canada. We have witnessed how Canadian laws have violated our treaties. We see all around us now the result of the violation of the treaties. Our people live in poverty because the treaties are not honoured. Our lands have not been transferred to us, and our rights have been unilaterally diminished. Collectively we must find the path for treaty justice.

To understand the importance of treaty justice we only need consider what happened to Big Bear and his people. I know something about the history of Treaty Six, not from living it, because I am from Treaty Five, but from reading about how it was made, and especially by reading about the life of Big Bear, a man for whom I have enormous admiration and respect. When Treaty Six was signed in 1876, Big Bear would not agree to his people joining. Why? Because he did not believe that the treaty was good for his people. He thought his people should be promised more, that their rights should be better protected. He did not sign the treaty the first time. Six years later, when the last buffalo were gone and Big Bear's people were starving, he signed Treaty Six. He did so because he wanted to ensure that the people would survive. Big Bear wanted to ensure his people had food and rations because it became impossible for them to fend for themselves, given the demise of the buffalo. He only did so because the Crown promised his people land and undertook to respect the rights of his people.

Big Bear opposed the poverty of the new reservations, which he said were inconsistent with the treaty promises. He was a man who wanted to bring unity to the Cree people and in 1884 he led a thirst dance of two thousand headmen at Chief Poundmaker's Reserve in Saskatchewan to foster unity. One year later, in 1885, during the rebellion in Western Canada, Big Bear's people were involved in defending their land. Something very wrong happened at Frog Lake, and some of Big Bear's warriors killed some Europeans. He tried to stop it, because he was a peacemaker and he always counselled for peace, but he was unsuccessful; some of his people were out of control. Because of this incident, Big Bear was sentenced to three years in prison for treason, at Stoney Mountain. A peaceful man, he looked out for the interests of his people, even while living the life of a prisoner with chains on his legs. They cut his hair short, and this was a personal indignity for him, because in the traditions of the Cree men at that time long hair was a respected symbol of authority and standing in Cree society. While he was in jail, what did the government do to his people, to his Cree brothers and sisters, who were members of Big Bear's Band? They dispersed them. They sent them off to different communities, and the reserve land that was set aside for Big Bear was taken away from them, and has never been restored.

His people live, right now, in different reserves in Alberta, Saskatchewan and in Montana. And they want some justice for this breach of their treaty.

When the reserve set aside for Big Bear was taken, what could his people do to protect their rights? They could do nothing because they had been dispersed. Their treaty was broken not more than six or seven years after it was signed. It is more than a hundred years now since Big Bear died, and since treaty lands were taken from him and his people. I think it is time we worked together to ensure that the reserve lands set aside under Treaty Six for Big Bear's people are restored.

When I was in Alberta recently, I went to the penitentiary in Edmonton to visit our people who are serving time for having committed various crimes. In the place where they meet as a brotherhood, one of the walls has pictures of two truly great Indian leaders, Big Bear and Poundmaker. Poundmaker went to jail with Big Bear for his involvement in the defence of his people during the Northwest Rebellion. So it should come as no great surprise to anyone that our brothers who are in prison would have these great men as their models. When I spoke to them, I said that when Big Bear came to prison, he had not committed a crime. He was a political prisoner. They understood what that meant.

Few of our people are political prisoners in the same sense as Big Bear. Still many of them are in jail simply because they are First Nations peoples and are therefore given harsher treatment in the criminal justice system.

Sometimes when I must make important presentations as the National Chief, I carry the medicine bundle that is attached to my office as a reminder of the importance of the position that I hold, and of my obligations to the peoples I represent. I want to represent my people in a way that offers dignity and does not dishonour anyone with whom I speak.

I also take it with me as an important lesson in history. The medicine bundle is part of the way of life for many First Nations in Canada. It is part of the connection that our people feel with the land and the Creator, and part of what makes us distinct from other societies that exist in Canada. It is not an historical artifact; it is a living and very vibrant aspect of our culture. I always think of Big Bear when I do this.

His medicine bundle is not with us because it is treated as an artifact and held in an American museum. After all the indignities his people suffered, his bundle is now a museum piece. I know from the life of Big Bear of the importance of showing respect to people and their distinct ways of life. Taking a piece of anyone's history, personality or identity and placing it in a museum to be observed by others, whoever they may be, is not an act of respect. It shows a complete disregard of the value our peoples place on the medicine bundles we carry. So I always remember Big Bear for all of these reasons.

In my own community, Grand Rapids, the Treaty Commissioners were told by my people when they came the very first time in 1870 that the paper they brought with them, Treaty Five, was not good enough, and they were sent away to get further instructions and return with something better. Two years later, the Treaty Commissioners came back with better promises and my ancestors signed Treaty Five. Even so, the reports of the Treaty Commissioners make it very clear that the Cree people resisted some of their ideas, and that they did not want to sign an agreement that did not protect their rights. They signed because they were promised a better future. When my people later read the treaty, it did not say what we had been promised. It did not represent what we understood were the commitments made to my people at treaty time.

Many years have passed since the signing of the Prairie treaties, but one thing remains constant: the better future we were promised, the lands and educa-tion and the hunting, trapping and fishing rights have not been delivered or honoured. Our understandings of our treaties have never become part of Canadian law, or been accepted or even respected by Canadian governments. Even the literal meaning of the written text has not been respected. We cannot wait another century before the rights promised in these treaties are enjoyed by our peoples. We need treaty justice.

The approach I propose we take for treaty justice is simple. We should seek only two things. First, we must move the terms of the treaties outside the realm of unilateral government interpretation, interference and betrayal. We have to stop the governments from continuing to pass laws that diminish our treaty rights. We believe that if one side wants to change the treaty, it should be discussed with the other side so that the consent of both parties is achieved. Second, we must ensure that the spirit and intent of the treaties—that is, the First Nations understandings of them—are given credence and respected by the Canadian governments and courts in implementing treaty promises. We need to be able to tell our stories about what our treaties mean; our oral histories about the treaty negotiations are as valid as the documents. These two points are very simple but putting them in place is a great battle. The governments do not want to deal with our treaties in any comprehensive or fair manner and have even tried to eliminate treaty rights over the years.

In the 1930s, after the provinces of Alberta, Saskatchewan and Manitoba were formed, they wanted land and resources. The Canadian government passed a law, the Natural Resources Transfer Agreement, without our consent, giving away our lands in Western Canada and limiting our treaty rights to hunt, fish and trap to harvesting for food only. This does not accord with the First Nations understanding of our treaties in those provinces; we were promised full enjoyment of our hunting rights and this included trade, too. As long as this law remains, our rights are diminished; they are at the whim of government. This is the treatment we have faced by Canada.

When you advocate something, there are two tendencies. One is to exaggerate and the other is to understate; it depends on the forum you are in. If you are in a political meeting, the rule of the game seems to be to exaggerate your position. But there are many lessons to show how this undermines your credibility and does not reach people. Understating your position is just as much a problem in my view. If you believe in something, say it and do not waver. State your position. First Nations peoples want their leaders to say something. We must stand for something, not just waffle on every issue and never answer to the people or express a view.

In 1992, I was invited to participate in a very important ceremony in the life of Treaty Six. I saw the RCMP, which is the symbol of the Canadian Crown, make its treaty payment to the people of Treaty Six— but that alone does not mean very much when the treaties are not respected to their full extent. There are many experiences in my life that have shaped or guided me. This gathering at Frog Lake was one of them. In their ceremony to renew the treaty agreement, the Elders unveiled the sacred Treaty Stem from its covering. It was the original Treaty Stem used in ceremonies when they signed Treaty Six back in 1876. It was broken in half. The Treaty Stem had been broken, just like the treaty promises have been broken. I do not know how the stem became broken. I do know how the treaties were broken, and that is that the government never fully honoured them.

Our peoples have been waiting a long time for the government to respect the treaties. The remarkable thing at Frog Lake was that the Elders prayed not for hatred or bitterness but for kindness. They prayed that Canadians would understand how important these treaties are for our peoples and that the First Nations peoples' relationship with Canada is based upon those treaties. They also prayed that the governments would find the wisdom to honour their treaty promises. Their prayers showed me the deep sense of victimization they feel as well as their enduring kindness in seeking a solution.

We have been arguing with governments, including the federal government, for many years now, but they are reluctant to do anything on treaties. I made it very clear that if there was no progress on treaty rights, there would be no progress on anything else in our discussions on the Canadian Constitution. I did that because it would be hypocritical for me to go to my people and say "trust the governments," when nothing has been done about the broken promises in the existing treaties. I told the governments that they must honour the treaties. They have to make sure that our people have the processes they need to sit down with governments to ensure we fully enjoy our treaty rights. This is required to build confidence in other changes and to develop goodwill.

When the treaty makers came to my own community of Grand Rapids, they spent a total of three hours there. It is difficult for me to believe that in three hours our people ceded all the land in the territory to the Canadian government. And yet that is what the text of the treaty states—that it was a total surrender of all lands and resources. Our oral understanding of these negotiations is that we agreed to share the lands. We were assured that our rights would be protected if we shared.

There is not a single living treaty Indian anywhere in Canada who has enjoyed his or her treaty rights to the fullest extent. We cannot wait for the government to change its views, because the longer we wait for treaty justice the less land there is, the fewer resources, and the more impossible it will become to ever fully enjoy our treaty rights. The longer we wait, the more time they have to do nothing. So if we keep waiting, we wait at our peril.

In the province of Saskatchewan, the Prime Minister signed an agreement in principle in 1992 to implement treaty land rights—almost one hundred years after the fact. Much remains to be done on this agreement. However, First Nations peoples in Saskatchewan may get some money to buy lands in lieu of their promised treaty lands. The fact that they were never given the lands promised to them in the treaties is very wrong. It is especially wrong when you consider that Indian people were forbidden until quite recently from going to the courts and fighting for our rights.

Some people have told me they have little confidence in new processes or in Canadian governments.

Some have told me they have no confidence in the Assembly of First Nations. After so many broken promises it is hard to have faith in new ones. I, too, have to live with my doubts about the ability of government to change its attitudes and its approaches. I want to be shown they are sincere, too. I did not create the problems we are facing, but I am trying to find a different way for them to be addressed. We must change this country, and we are struggling to change it in a fundamental way. The full impact of our efforts will not be known for a while. But when I see the young people of today, I hope they will not have to spend their adult lives fighting for their treaty rights just as Harold Cardinal, Victor Buffalo, Chief Antoine and so many others before them have done.

# Let the Curtain Fall on the Indian Act

*The Indian Act is a quagmire for Canada. It has been condemned as racist and colonial and held out in the international community as a huge blight on Canada's human rights record. The legacy is significant because the Act is almost as old as Canada itself; it has origins in colonial and Canadian law dating back to 1876, and has been revised twice in a major way, first in 1951 and more recently in 1985.*

*For the past one hundred years, every study, report or review of First Nations-Canadian relations has come to the same conclusion: the 'Big Brother' Indian Act is an unacceptable basis for the relations between First Nations and Canada. It has been such a powerful force in the lives of First Nations individuals and communities that it is hard to give a snapshot of how it rules and undermines. Coming to grips with it as First Nations people is difficult; we can hardly imagine life without it because it is all we've ever known.*

*The Act is a cradle-to-grave set of rules, regulations and directives. From the time of birth, when an Indian child must be registered in one of seventeen categories defining who is an "Indian," until the time of death, when the Minister of Indian Affairs acts as executor of the deceased person's estate, our lives are ruled by the Act and the overwhelming bureaucracy that administers it. The alien form of government the Act has imposed requires that Band Councils be elected to govern the affairs of Indian people. Parliament has issued regulations stating how elections are to be conducted and defining the terms and conditions of Band Council membership. The Act spells out in no uncertain terms the severely limited scope of Band Council powers. For example, a Band Council can pass laws to deal with bee-keeping and noxious weeds, but not with child welfare.*

*All by-laws passed by Band Councils must be submitted to the Minister of Indian Affairs for approval before they can come into force. The Minister has forty days to allow or disallow each by-law and disapprovals are routine. The Minister is under no obligation to provide reasons why a law was disallowed. For example, a by-law to control dogs might be approved for one reserve but not another, according to whether the bureaucrats in the*

Department of Indian Affairs liked it during the forty-day
review period. All this results in an inconsistent pattern
across the country and frustration on the part of Council
members. And efforts to address important social problems
through new policies or legal frameworks can be wasted if the
Minister of Indian Affairs does not countenance the work
done by the Band Council. The Indian Act represents
something very different than self-government. It is other-
government, and the other in this case is the Department of
Indian Affairs and its Minister.

Many people have been excluded from First Nations
communities because of the history of discrimination against
certain people under the Indian Act. For example, women
lost their Indian status if they married people who were
considered non-Indians, even though their spouses may also
have been discriminated against by the Indian Act. Many
women lost their official status and with it the right to live on
the reserve with their families. They also lost the right to
have their children attend schools on the reserve and the
ability to be part of their community so they could sustain
their language and culture. But women were not the only
ones excluded. People who went to university or joined the
clergy or armed forces were also removed from the Indian
register. And many people whose families were out on the
land when the enumerators came around were just left off
the list.

*While some of this discrimination was remedied through a 1985 amendment to the Indian Act, many kinds of discrimination remain and new forms have been created. The bitterness of that experience is profound. It is also a critical part of the dynamic of First Nations politics. Those who have been excluded feel strongly aggrieved by Canada and also by their own communities, many of which have been slow to welcome returning citizens. Some bands have said that they cannot allow all the newly registered people to return because of a lack of housing, schools and other services for this new population due to an absence of government funding. Many people remain excluded.*

*People who have registered as Indians since 1985 and are not members of a particular band, or who are still considered "non-status," are not represented by the Assembly of First Nations, since it is an organization of Chiefs and status or registered Indians. Even still, these people are family members and neat distinctions derived from the Indian Act are not thicker than water. The rifts that do exist between the Chiefs and newly registered or non-status Indians are significant and ways are being sought to bridge them. In a sense, these problems can be traced directly to the Indian Act, yet it is now up to First Nations peoples to overcome more than a century of division. One way to do this is for First Nations to take direct control over citizenship and residence.*

*Issues of trust arise whenever First Nations communities talk about the future because the Indian Act has been such a negative force. Many First Nations peoples have little trust in their own local governments because the Indian Act has allowed a situation to occur where some Band Councils make arbitrary decisions and are not fully accountable to the people. They are accountable instead to the Minister of Indian Affairs. For example, suppose the Chief and Councillors decide to allocate new housing to relatives instead of to those who are most in need: individual First Nations citizens have little recourse to challenge such decisions because the Council's accountability is first to the Department of Indian Affairs and second to the people. This is not to say that Chiefs and all Councils behave irresponsibly but that the Indian Act through this imposed structure of government leaves the door open to unaccountable acts.*

●●●

When we initiated the most recent part of our campaign for self-government, we were advised by the Elders to keep it simple. We were told to keep our objective in mind and work steadily towards it. We were cautioned not to get sidetracked or distracted by the inevitable political disagreements and disappointments. They said our objective was to broaden the reach of our friendships and to begin to address, finally, the just demands of the Aboriginal peoples. This must include addressing, in a far-reaching way, the single biggest obstacle in our path, the Indian Act.

If we are really to change this country, we must find new principles, very different from those embodied in the Indian Act, to guide our relations with the governments of Canada and with Canadian citizens. Aboriginal peoples can no longer be excluded from decisions made about this country and we can no longer be passive bystanders in decisions made about our lives. The First Nations of Canada should not be continually placed in the position where we have to fight for our basic collective rights, for our very existence in our own country. But if we are excluded from the political structure of Canada, and kept under the thumb of the Department of Indian Affairs, we will have to resist; we will have to fight against other agendas and priorities. So how do we avoid this disharmony? How do we avoid confrontations? We avoid them by adopting, as a basic principle for Canada, collective rights of different peoples and especially First Peoples. This will take us beyond the Indian Act.

With the speed of transportation and the variety of communications in the modern world, we come into contact more frequently than our ancestors did with non-Aboriginal peoples. This is part of who we are now, too. We live with the newcomers and that will never be reversed. But what needs to be reversed is the ignorance about our peoples. When we meet non-Aboriginal people socially, there is often a gap, a lack of understanding of who we are. I have seen it first-hand in my travels. People are uncomfortable with us; they don't know how to react because they do not understand where we are coming from and what we are seeking.

One of the reasons we worked so hard on constitutional reform was that we saw the Constitution as a vital instrument to create bridges and friendships and to break down the barriers between First Nations and Canadian society. We thought that constitutional reform would allow us to enjoy basic rights that Canadian people take for granted but do not extend to us. Canadian people know the importance of collective rights, of democracy. We have collective rights too, but they are not recognized or fully accepted by the laws of this country. We believe we have a right to be different. We belong here. We should not be forced to assimilate. There is no need for us to look the same or act the same for there to be a just society. Sameness is not a prerequisite of national unity. A vital and strong society that respects collective differences can exist. Difference is not something to be afraid of but something to embrace, something to respect in a progressive nation-state. Our whole relationship with Canada has been based on our exclusion from politics. Ending exclusion is a crucial political goal; to achieve it, we must deal with the Indian Act.

You see, I know what exclusion feels like. I've lived it. Just before my election as National Chief I was given status as what is called a "Bill C-31 Indian," although I would never define myself in that humiliating way. Bill C-31 was the 1985 amendment to the Indian Act. It was supposed to overturn some of the discrimination in the Act, including the kind which excluded my family from being considered Indians. I was excluded because my mother married George Mercredi, a Métis trapper who did not have Indian status. Before 1985, if an Indian woman married a non-Indian she lost her status as an Indian person and her children were not considered Indians. Yet if a man did the same thing, he did not lose his status and his children were recognized. In fact, according to the Act, his non-Indian wife could legally become an Indian person. So my mother was stripped of her status and so were her children. This is what the Indian Act does — it makes arbitrary bureaucratic distinctions about one's identity. I am a Cree. That is how I was raised, that is who I am, and I will never let that federal Act define me. We must resist its humiliating categories. That Act will not allow my daughter,

Danielle, to be accepted either, because of leftover sex discrimination that makes grandchildren of my mother ineligible for registration as Indians. So even after Bill C-31 my daughter is still not an Indian in Canada. We must fight so that those like her are not excluded from our communities.

We have this peculiar past where legislation was passed by Parliament in 1876 to define who is, and who is not, an Indian. The 1985 amendment, which was intended to be an improvement, defines seventeen different categories of Indian. We have seen other legislation like this in Nazi Germany and South Africa. Part of our struggle is to ensure that the kind of pain that the Indian Act has imposed on us will not be repeated, and this is why we are so concerned about the inherent right to self-government. We must be the ones who determine who is and who is not a member of our community, based on criteria accepted by our people. A good example is the approach of the Dene people in the North. For them, membership requires family connection, a knowledge of Dene culture and language, and a commitment to the good of the people. For them, identity is not based on race but on culture and family; it reflects their Dene values.

What is especially hurtful about the Indian Act is that while we did not make it, nor have we ever consented to it, it has served to divide our peoples. We sometimes buy into Indian Act definitions and categories in our own assessments of people and politics. This is part of the legacy of colonialism. When Parliament tried to correct its mistakes in 1985, it exacerbated them instead. What else could be expected of a law imposed on us by the federal government? All it did was reinstate the obvious persons who were rejected, but it did not make it possible within Canadian law for me to transfer my identity to my daughter. It is still up to someone else to decide who is or is not Indian. In fact, there is still a person in Ottawa called the Registrar whose job it is to decide who's in and who's out. The power is still with the bureaucrats to tell us who is or is not a Cree person.

Because of the power the Indian Act exerts over our peoples and the injustice it causes, our authority and power as First Nations citizens and governments have been undermined. The Act has imposed a municipal style of government in the form of Band Councils with the result that our traditional government systems and values have been seriously compromised and in some cases lost. For example, in the Iroquois custom of the "Haudenosaunee" or Longhouse, the clan mothers select the chiefs or headmen. They follow an elaborate set of important rules for assigning political responsibility within a spiritual context. Though it is contrary to the Indian Act, the Longhouse government still thrives in some Iroquois communities. Yet to Canadian governments, the Longhouse garners no recognition or respect; they will deal only with the Band Councils. This results in internal divisions which can be so powerful that they lead to violence and factionalism in our communities.

We want to revive the traditions of consensus decision-making that involve everyone. Consensus democracy means that responsibility is put back where it belongs—in the hands of our people. But the Indian Act has dictated a style of government that has forced our peoples to adopt what I call the ten-second model of democracy, since it gives us input at the ballot box for a total of about ten seconds every few years. We have gotten used to a style of government that does not reflect our tradition of fully involving the people.

Some of our people have become so accustomed to having no responsibility for their lives that the idea of self-government frightens them, and this is a tragedy. A few even see the Indian Act as our only protection. In order to survive and make progress, we must recognize and break out of the patterns of dependency taught to us under the dominance of Parliament. We cannot survive and make progress under the totalitarian rule of the

Indian Affairs bureaucracy; we have to do it through the free will of our peoples.

We have to learn to trust each other and rebuild from the Indian Act experience. We have to look carefully at how we have been affected by that legislation and trust that we will do the right thing for our people. I know some people do not want to put blind faith or trust in any governments, not even Aboriginal governments, after all they have seen. I do not blame them. But I have more faith in my people to govern than I do in the Department of Indian Affairs. Our traditional values were undermined by the Indian Act, and our people are trying to reclaim them in order to chart a better future. If our new governments reflect our values and incorporate our traditions, then that trust can be regained.

Some people do not trust our Chiefs with power. They believe power will lead the Chiefs to create Indian Act-style governments which work only in the interests of the federal government. Some people believe that if our inherent right of self-government is enshrined, we will abuse the power and mistreat First Nations citizens. But I believe we will use the power for the public good, for peaceful and effective government of our peoples. I have great faith in our ability to build something better after everything we have survived. We have the will, the knowledge and the skill to break out of the Indian Act for good.

Whatever we do in the future to implement our inherent right of self-government, we must ensure that one basic thing happens: that any change in governance is consented to by those who are affected by it. Our people must choose how to combine traditions with contemporary needs and obligations. The consent of the Minister of Indian Affairs, the Prime Minister, or the provincial premier should not be the deciding factor. Our peoples must be the ones to decide.

Let me use a specific example to make clear what we are seeking. Like other communities in Canada, First Nations communities have problems with child abuse, physical and sexual abuse, and alcohol and solvent abuse. These must be dealt with by our people in our own ways, not by government agencies or social workers. The healing has to come from our people or it will not work. Outside support may be welcomed, but it must not be imposed. Our people have to be in control of protecting our children from abuse in the future. Right now, under the Indian Act, the Chiefs and the Councillors and the people on the reserves have no authority to deal with this issue in a comprehensive way. The Indian Act does not allow us the power to make decisions about our own children. When we try to run programs to promote child welfare the federal government says we have no business doing so because it is an area of provincial jurisdiction. But when we turn to the province, its representatives tell us it is a federal responsibility and they can do nothing to help. This jurisdictional confusion can be dealt with very quickly by recognizing our inherent right to self-government. Then we would no longer need to run to the federal or provincial government to seek permission to do what is in the best interests of our children. Once our authority is recognized, our people will be able to do something about the lives of our children.

It must be remembered that there is an important distinction between self-determination and self-administration. One means we design our own institutions and rely on our own values, the other that we apply someone else's programs. The Department of Indian Affairs would have us embrace the second option, they even dress it up and try to sell it as self-government to Indian bands, but it is self-determination that we seek. A First Nations government must have the political authority to decide what programs to provide, at what levels and under what conditions to provide them, and by what process, if any, to charge constituents for services. A First Nations government must be able to decide whether to establish its own standards or whether to follow provincial standards for services like health care and education. In some cases, provincial standards don't apply. In education, for example, we need a combination of First Nations and provincial curricula in order to teach First Nations languages, customs, traditions and history. We are not saying we want to create new approaches in isolation from Canadian people and governments, but that we need authority in the process, too.

Economic development and self-government must grow together so that greater political authority can be accompanied by increased economic and administrative self-sufficiency. A government with a very limited economic base cannot be truly autonomous so we need to achieve justice in our lands and resources negotiations with Canada. We must find fairer ways for sharing in the wealth of this land and dealing with the poverty our peoples have experienced. We must plan for a future of economic security for our children and grandchildren and we must do this with a generous heart. This means big changes. It certainly means something other than the Indian Act system we have lived under for more than one hundred years, and that something isn't self-administration.

We can never be truly self-governing under a form of government delegated by Parliament. The inherent right to govern means that we do not need Parliament's permission to run our own affairs, although we have a political relationship with the Crown through our governments. It means that our rights come from our own people, our own past; they cannot be delegated from the federal or provincial governments as some kind of handout. We will not allow some other society to decide what we can do and determine the limits of our authority.

I am often asked whether it would be better to change the existing Indian Act or to eliminate it entirely. Will we still need the Indian Act once our right to self-government is recognized and our treaties are implemented? I believe we will need some federal legislation to make clear the obligations the federal government bears towards First Nations peoples. This is radically different from an Indian Act that continues to allow a minister and some bureaucrats to tell people who they are, what they can do, or how they must live. That arrangement is a colonial relic. We would all like to see it disappear. But we would like to see the government fulfill its responsibilities to us, not shirk them by repealing the Indian Act and pretending that is the end of their obligations to First Peoples.

# Individual Rights and Collective Responsibilities

The Indian Act is deeply resented because it has been imposed. Typically, Parliament or a provincial legislature simply steps into what it perceives as a problem and resolves it by passing unilateral legislation or issuing new policies. This pattern has almost wholly destroyed the potential for joint First Nations-Canada responses to problems.

The imposition of the Canadian Charter of Rights and Freedoms on Indian communities in 1982 continued this pattern. Canadian governments approved the Charter without First Nations input or consent. The Charter is a very contentious law because it is all about values. And since there was no opportunity for First Nations input, the values reflected in it are not always shared by First Nations peoples or emphasized in the way we would consider appropriate. For example, many First Nations peoples are not comfortable with the Charter's adversarial approach of *dealing with conflicts in the court system. Others challenge the Charter's interpretation of rights as weapons to be used against governments; we tend to see rights as collective responsibilities instead of individual rights—or at least see the strong link between the two.*

*The Indian Act is part and parcel of the controversy over the Charter for two reasons. First, both were imposed unilaterally by government. Second, the government wants to apply the Charter to solve the human rights problems it created when it imposed the Indian Act. Many First Nations people question why we should allow government to impose more unilateral legislation as a way of solving the problems they generated in the first place.*

It is very important for people to understand that we are not opposed to the idea of a Charter, we are opposed to the imposition of the Canadian Charter of Rights and Freedoms on our peoples, which was prepared and adopted without our input. We recognize that all governments have to respect individual rights and that Aboriginal governments are no exception. We do not propose to disrespect this. But the Canadian Charter is not appropriate for us. We have our own approaches. One option to deal with individual rights within our institutions and governments is to create Aboriginal

Charters that would apply to Aboriginal institutions and governments. These Charters would reflect our values, customs and aspirations. They would also reflect our own way of dealing with disputes so they can be kept out of Canadian courts and away from the adversarial process.

To help people understand the basis of our resistance to the current Charter, I will give some examples. But first let me make it clear that it has nothing to do with wanting to undermine or diminish women. We are not opposed to gender equality. We are not opposed to the individual freedom and choice of any First Nations citizen. We want to guard against the destruction of traditional forms of governing ourselves and ways of resolving disputes. We cannot do this without the full involvement of women.

The hereditary system of self-government in British Columbia, for example, is not based on democratic principles of a parliamentary system of government, meaning one vote per person. A hereditary system is based on certain families taking responsibility for aspects of community life.

In restoring ourselves as peoples, it is very important that we are not forced to emulate European-style, democratically elected governments, since traditional forms of government may be the only way to ensure the recovery of our communities and our peoples. Democracy means more than just voting. Hereditary systems, with direct consultation and involvement with the people, are also democratic. The traditional Chiefs from each of the families deliberate on political matters. Our traditional forms of government are based on the consent of the people. The Charter must not interfere with the recovery of our traditional forms of government, or it will complete the job the Indian Act started.

In 1925, the RCMP raided the Six Nations Confederacy Longhouse and forced out the Confederacy government. It was replaced with an electoral system under the Indian Act. But the Confederacy is still in existence. It has never been extinguished, and the people who support that form of self-government want it to continue for an indefinite period of time. Under the clan system, Indian men don't vote; the leader is chosen by the women of that society, and only the women. We want it to be possible for the Confederacy to continue, and perhaps emerge as an even stronger force for dealing with the social and economic ills that exist in our communities.

In the province of Manitoba, the people of the Roseau River First Nation are reinstating the Midewin Lodge government. They have thrown out the electoral system under the Indian Act and are using what they call custom as a basis for selecting leadership. The custom they have revived is a clan system, based on their view that the heads of the various clans select the heads of government. Because this system is not based on one person, one vote elections, it runs contrary to the provisions of the Charter in terms of individual rights and democratic rights.

In northern Manitoba, at the Ste. Theresa Reserve, the Chief and Council set up their own juvenile court because they wanted social control in the community and they were worried about their young people being out of control. They didn't do it pursuant to any provisions in the Constitution; they did it as a matter of their own right to do it. They don't allow lawyers into the court because they want to deal with the issue of juvenile delinquency in a traditional way, using a healing circle and focusing on harmony and rehabilitation. As it operates right now, the Ste. Theresa system likely violates the Charter because legal counsel is not allowed even though the Charter guarantees legal counsel to accused persons. If someone were to challenge it, the courts might not have any alternative but to enforce the Charter, and one more source of hope for using traditional values in dealing with social problems would disappear.

The traditions of the Ojibwa peoples and the Midewin spirituality don't separate politics and religion. They incorporate both those ideas as part of their way of dealing with the needs of their people and their society. Our ways of dealing with juvenile delinquents are very effective—more effective than can be expected from a fly-in court of white judges and lawyers. I know, because I've travelled with those courts. We use the Elders to deal with the source of the problem, not just the symptoms, and to correct the imbalances in the community by healing both the victims and the offenders. The focus is on healing and restoration, not the adversarial process and punishment.

The Charter imposes a particular point of view on how justice should be administered on behalf of Canadians, and it doesn't include our communal vision. It usually involves a Crown attorney, a judge, a defence counsel, recording people, corrections facilities, group homes and obviously jails. Our traditional forms of justice do not have to duplicate these practices. We should have the freedom to establish forms of justice that will be acceptable to and workable for our people. We have to tailor them to our social problems, not to the interests of others.

The primary objective of the Charter is to protect individual freedoms, but Aboriginal peoples have individual freedoms through our own forms of government. Who is to say that freedom of conscience and religion, freedom of thought and belief, and freedom of association do not exist in our societies? Of course they exist. We believe in maximizing individual autonomy without sacrificing a sense of community responsibility. Our beliefs and values do not exist because the Canadian Charter says they exist. Our societies and cultures are older than Canada's. Our values are part of who we are. The suggestion that we lack these attributes or that our values are wrong or inferior because they are not the same is insulting. The truth is that our basis for governing our lives has been more consensual than Canada's. It is more directly democratic. Canada's idea of democracy is majority rule. Our idea of running governments is consensus by the people. Who is to say that Canada's principles are better than ours?

When it comes to individual rights, Canadian society, in principle, is a very good society. However, Aboriginal peoples and people of colour in Canada don't always enjoy those individual rights. The courts are expensive and slow and the Charter has fallen short of its objective of creating equality in terms of individual rights. I've been to four penitentiaries in the last ten months. I wonder, when I see these young Indian men, how the legal rights provisions in the Charter have ensured their freedom or protected their individual rights within a criminal system where we are grossly overrepresented.

The Charter should not be seen as a panacea for the ills of society. If the government plans to impose its solution to its problems on us, we will resist. We want the scope to do things in a way that works. It is in this context that we have argued against the Charter, not because we are opposed to individual rights as a matter of policy. And it has absolutely nothing to do with resistance to gender equality, even though some would present it this way. Where did our gender inequality come from? From the Indian Act, and not from our traditions.

I cannot accept the idea that we have to take the Charter or have no self-government. It should not be a "take it or leave it" situation. The Charter was imposed without seriously considering whether it is appropriate for us or what its impact might be. The Chiefs cannot accept the Charter without some conditions to preserve our identity and rights. Canada cannot ask us to condemn our traditional forms of government. We are not prepared to do this, because our traditional values are our hope.

Those who have not experienced life under the Indian Act cannot understand why we react the way we do, with the strong emotions that we feel when we are told how to live, how to be civilized, that our ways are inferior. How can they know what it is like to live under a system with no opportunity to determine the future? I realize that it is difficult for non-Aboriginal people to understand that our traditional forms of government are as fair as an electoral system, but I have lived in both societies. I understand both ways, and ours is not inferior or undemocratic.

The Indian Act has been used historically to deny our people our own identity. The result of this dominance over our peoples' lives is very present in the minds of many of us right now. We have a strong sense of victimization and many grievances. Every time we see the exercise of that dominance again, as in the Charter debate, we react as I do, with a sense of indignation. We do not want to see our rights or identity suppressed or denied. We want to guarantee the rights of our peoples so they can have some freedom, something they do not enjoy under the Canadian parliamentary system of government.

First Nations peoples have to protect our languages, our culture and our identity because these reflect who we are. Who would argue otherwise? Our identities have been unwelcome in Canadian institutions of education. We were told we could not speak our languages there. The reason only three of the fifty-two Aboriginal languages in Canada might survive in the next century is because they have not been protected in

the way that the English and French languages have.
We will guard our languages for our future generations;
how can anyone ask us to do otherwise?

The Charter that Canadians cherish and embrace,
that has existed for just over ten years, has not
improved the rights of my peoples in the Canadian system of government or society. The guarantee of freedom of thought does not seem to exist when it comes
to traditional religion. Every time our Elders pass
through customs they are challenged because they hold
religious items that are not common knowledge to customs officers. While we may not have benefited as
Indian people from the Canadian Charter of Rights
and Freedoms or Canadian human rights legislation,
we do know the importance of individual rights. But
our struggle is only partially about individual rights in
Canada. It is about finding acceptance in Canadian
cities so that we are not rejected simply because we are
First Nations peoples. For a long time now our peoples
have been excluded, for no apparent reason, from
being equal members of Canadian society. I do not
mean individual equality where I can run for office in
your legislature or I can become a landlord in this city
or I can use your public services free from discrimination. These are important things but they are individual rights.

What we want is recognition of our collective rights. We see ourselves as distinct peoples with inherent rights which exist because of our history on this land, this place we collectively refer to as Turtle Island. For the life of me, I do not understand why my people have been excluded from shaping the country in a fundamental way. Our art, our music, our ceremonies are part of the essence of Canada. But we are excluded on the political front. We look to Quebec with a sense of pride for French Canadians, but also with a certain amount of jealousy for the political security they enjoy.

Do not expect us to be champions of the Canadian Charter when there is no evidence that it can help our people and when it is being imposed without debate. Perhaps if it were applied more generously it would result in some positive legal rights for our people. Maybe then we would be more sympathetic to arguments that it should apply to us. But in the meantime do not expect us to accept it.

Newly elected National Chief Ovide Mercredi rises to greet the Chiefs
at the Winnipeg Convention Centre on June 12, 1991. The Chiefs
accepted his vision of political strength through traditional values like
respect, compassion, understanding and sharing.

Ovide explains the Canadian Constitution to Innu children at their school in Labrador. He describes how First Nations peoples have been overlooked by the Canadian political system and how this can be changed.

Ovide greeting children at the Montagnais community in Sept-Isles, Quebec in September 1991.

He travels extensively to learn first-hand about community problems and to develop a strategy for bringing concerns to the national stage.

The National Chief invited The Right Honourable Joe Clark to a gathering of Chiefs at Morley, Alberta, in July 1991. There they developed a friendly and respectful understanding of each other's aspirations and political limitations.

*Top:* Ovide with his spouse, Shelley Buhay, and their friends A.J. and Pat Felix, in Northern Saskatchewan.

*Bottom:* Ovide dances in Prince Albert, Saskatchewan, after receiving his headdress from Chiefs and Elders in the Tribal Council. The headdress accompanies him during his travels as National Chief.

Ovide outside the Prime Minister's residence at 24 Sussex Drive,
Ottawa. He had been excluded from a meeting of the Prime Minister
and the premiers.

*Top:* There was a jubilant rally on Parliament Hill on July 14, 1992, to celebrate progress during constitutional discussions. To the right of the National Chief is Elder Sandy Beardy of Cross Lake, Manitoba, one of the National Chief's advisors.

*Bottom:* Ovide, his mother and father and young cousin Jacob Cook, at his home community of Grand Rapids, Manitoba.

Chuck Stoody/CANAPRESS

Brian Willer

*Top:* The National Chief shares a laugh with British Columbia Vice-Chief Wendy Grant at Squamish. Vice-Chief Grant was hosting a meeting of the Chiefs to review the Charlottetown Accord and share ideas on the Referendum.

*Bottom:* Ovide and his daughter, Danielle Mercredi, at Six Nations Reserve School in September 1991.

Bill Glaister

Ovide with Rosemary Kuptana, President of the Inuit Tapirisat of Canada. Their close friendship forged a strong political alliance between Inuit and First Nations Organizations.

Fred Chartrand/CANAPRESS

Ovide talks with Elijah Harper on the progress of constitutional discussions. They worked closely during the Meech Lake Accord debate and still share views on national issues.

Ovide visits the St. Regis Freedom School in July 1992 to meet with the next generation of leaders.

Ovide poses with friends and advisors just after his naming ceremony led by the Elders in Fredericton, New Brunswick in June 1992. From left to right: Harold Tarbell (with arm around Justin Monture–Okanee), Richard Powless, Mary Ellen Turpel (holding the paddle the Elders have just given Ovide) and Roger Jones.

The authors address the Quebec National Assembly Committee on Quebec Sovereignty. The mood was tense after the Committee refused to allow the Chiefs and Elders to bring a drum into the Assembly. Eventually the Committee relented and the presentation proceeded.

Chuck Stoody/CANAPRESS

Louise Labrie

*Above:* Ovide receives encouragement from Elder Flora Tababadung after a turbulent meeting of the Chiefs in Vancouver. Seated with him are Chief Ed John (left) and Chief Lyndsay Cyr.

*Right:* Ovide meets with Nobel Laureate and Guatemalan Indian Rigoberta Menchu at the Ottawa offices of the Assembly of First Nations. Ovide is Rigoberta's North American ambassador.

Ovide attends the 1992 Remembrance Day services at the Ottawa War
Memorial. In 1991 he had to crash the event to bring attention to the
record of Indian Veterans, but this time he was invited, as was the
National Indian Veterans Association.

# Self-Government as a Way to Heal

Most Canadians have witnessed the movement for the recognition of the inherent right of self-government through debates over the Meech Lake and Charlottetown Accords. Long before these recent debates, special inquiries into self-government generated countless studies, reports and recommendations. The Royal Commission on Aboriginal Peoples, due to report in 1995, is currently engaged in many more studies on this issue.

The concept of self-government is confusing for many people because we have not had sufficient opportunity to explain what we mean by it. But it is really a very simple concept: First Nations peoples governing ourselves in keeping with our values, customs and traditions and not being ruled by the Minister of Indian Affairs or the Department of Indian Affairs. Our motivation for self-government is equally simple: self-preservation. We believe that Indian self-government is the only way to survive and flourish, given the powerful tide of assimilation that has been our history.

First Nations governments would not be cut off or isolated from federal, provincial or municipal governments. As a practical matter, all governments have to coordinate their efforts and their respective jurisdictions. The image that some critics may have created of a "Swiss Cheese" Canada with pockets of independent republics is far-fetched and destructive. People have to live and work together within agreed upon terms.

Criticisms of self-government often stem from the accurate observation that Indian people do not do things the way non-Aboriginal Canadians do. Different political ideas are often seen as inferior, and critics have trouble accepting the legitimacy of doing things in a way that does not conform to the status quo. The message First Nations peoples get loud and clear from this kind of criticism is: "Do not act like a First Nations person and you will get ahead. Do not speak your language and you will do well at school. Civilize. Overcome your inferiority and you can grow up and be just as good as Canadians." The sting of this message—reinforced in so many ways in Canadian society, from the school system through to the Indian Act—is vicious. It leaves people feeling inferior, even starting to believe that such cruel and ignorant criticisms are true. The presumption that anything First Nations peoples do is savage and sub-standard causes anger. It is all we can do to control this anger, having been dictated to for so long about the inferiority of First Nations peoples. Self-government is a way of saying our governments can be different without being inferior in any way.

At a certain point First Nations people get tired of explaining what self-government means, especially when it seems that the questions are asked simply so the answers can be attacked. And First Nations views on the issue are diverse and dynamic. For self-government to really mean something to Canadians, it has to be explained by First Nations peoples in a non-adversarial setting. This is one of the purposes of this book: to build bridges of understanding so that the fact of self-government will be accepted, and so that the attitude of superiority that is at the root of how First Nations peoples are treated in Canada will finally be removed. It is also clear that self-government does not materialize overnight. It is premised on a new partnership with Canada and the transition away from the Indian Act.

●●●

Many people seem to hold the idea that the only governments in Canada are the federal and provincial governments. There is still much work to be done before we can convince our Canadian brothers and sisters that we

are their equals and our governments are part of
Canada. I do not mean equals in a sense of individual
equality. I mean equals in the context of collective
rights, in the context of our peoples not being seen as
inferior peoples possessing inferior governments. This
relationship of equality is what our treaties were based
on—respect for each other. These treaties are still alive
today.

Since the signing of the treaties, we have sometimes forgotten their significance. Canadians have forgotten that the treaties have to be interpreted according
to our understanding, too. Along the way, they have
forgotten to look upon our people as collectives with
inherent rights that existed prior to their arrival; they
have seen us as inferior and beneath them. We have
contributed to this thinking by accepting too quietly
the Indian Act instead of insisting on our right to govern ourselves. We allowed the Department of Indian
Affairs to run our peoples' lives. We did so because we
are kind and trusting peoples. We want to have good
relations. That trust has been broken.

We have a duty as the original people of this country to restore our traditions, to advocate for our rights,
and to do it in a way that is consistent with our sovereignty and our contemporary needs. That is what the
inherent right of self-government means: correcting an

imbalance that exists between us and the rest of
Canada. The inherent right is not a battle cry for power.
It is a cry for the reformation of Canada. It is a demand
for the reclamation of our inherent sovereignty as distinct peoples within Canada, to make this a better
nation.

The inherent right to govern ourselves has more
than just symbolic value. It is a clear statement to the
rest of Canada that we are reasserting our place in this
country; we are doing it on our terms and we are doing
it in a peaceful way that respects your institutions, that
respects you as individuals, and that respects your governments. If we can create a new relationship that elim-
inates the dominance of one society over ours, we will
eliminate prejudice, stereotyping and discrimination.
We will not only gain in terms of the economic wealth
of Canada, in terms of its lands and resources, but we
will also get rid of the psychology of inferiority that
affects the minds and hearts of so many of our own people. When you stop being controlled by the Indian Act
and you start living as a free man or a free woman, you
stand tall on the heritage of your people. You act with
the pride of your nation and with the strength to control your own destiny. You are not inferior to anybody.
That is the vital symbolic importance of the inherent
right of self-government.

The inherent right is not about power, but fundamentally about responsibility. When it is officially recognized, we will have a major challenge to implement it in a way that does justice to our people, brings about healing in our communities and is respectful of the Earth. We have to accept our responsibilities. We must begin to make the critical decisions for our people like how we should provide for children who are in need of protection or, for that matter, how we are going to provide for the health or education needs of our communities. We must make these decisions with fairness, compassion and understanding.

I have visited many, many Indian reservations in all parts of Canada. I make these trips for two reasons: one is to understand the needs and the problems of First Nations and to try to appreciate the diversity of our people. The second is to try to build unity, because without the strength of common purpose, we will not be able to advance the rights of our people.

Part of our job is to make ourselves stronger and to make each other stronger. I've wondered how we can do that. I am coming slowly to the realization that power politics does not make people strong. Power politics in our communities and organizations will not heal our people; if anything, it may create more problems and divide our people. Our leaders have to be more than just typical politicians. But to get there we have to escape the Indian Act thinking and recapture the traditions and the values of our societies. Each of us has been the victim of assimilation, and yet none of us is fully integrated into Canadian society. We cannot be comfortable with that. There is always something left inside of ourselves that is rooted in our traditions and identity as First Nations. You can see this in the way we relate to each other as human beings, and in the way we must conduct ourselves as leaders.

What impresses me about traditional values is how simple they are—how simple, and yet how difficult to apply in the world of politics and in our struggles with government. For example, the principle of respect is a very simple requirement of human relations, though it is difficult to achieve in our relationships with Canadian society when we do not feel respected by others. Kindness is also a very simple principle. It goes a long way to healing people. We were taught at least those two basic principles—respect and kindness—from the time we were crawling to the time we left our parents' homes. If we apply these traditional values among ourselves, in our work and our communities, we will not have to talk about unity because it will just exist by virtue of the way we relate to each other.

These traditions may be difficult to apply because

most of us have become too individualistic and do not value our Elders enough. We are having trouble maintaining our sense of community because we think not so much about the needs of others but about our own personal needs and advancement. We must resist this selfishness and re-evaluate individualism. The idea that individual rights are superior to collective rights—an idea we learned from White society—is creating imbalance and confusion in our communities. If we are going to restore our traditional values, we have to do it first and foremost in the context of our relationships with each other.

Our ability to come together in the community will depend on our sense of responsibility for the group. It is as simple as that. Progress as individuals does not guarantee progress as a group; some people will be left behind. Individualism is, by its very nature in a capitalistic society, nothing more than survival of those who are most competitive. I am not advocating the return of society as it was in 1867 or before. Our traditional values are just as valid today as they were in 1867 and they will be just as valid for us in the year 2067. Values transcend historical periods, they move through time with us. They are as dynamic as our peoples. We have an opportunity to remain as distinct peoples if we choose to focus on these values.

The challenge for our peoples is to determine how we can heal ourselves. How much confidence do we have in our own way of doing things? How willing are we to sacrifice our individual advancement for the sake of the community? I do not want anyone to think for one moment that the inherent right of self-government alone is going to solve the problems we have suffered. It is not. We, as individuals working together for the interests of a common good, can move ahead. We are the ones who are going to make the difference. The choices we make must not be individual choices but those of a community, made with the full input of all our citizens.

There are many issues to consider regarding self-government. The first one is what kind of governments do we want? Do we want governments with power that is unfettered, with no checks and balances? Do we want governments that will operate under the Canadian Charter of Rights and Freedoms according to the values of Canadian society? Do we need codes of ethics for our leaders? Traditional society was based upon the principle of consensus for government, but discipline, including political discipline, was there too. Consensus must be the most perfect form of democracy known because it means that there is no imposition of the rule of the majority. Everyone has input and no one is excluded because of some provision in the Indian Act. We do not want to repeat the rule of the majority we have experienced under Canadian law.

We also have to ask ourselves, when rebuilding our communities and restructuring our societies, what kind of society do our people seek, right now and for the future? One conclusion is inescapable: no government can function properly if it does not respect individuals and accord them protection and participation in government. There is no sense in trying to refute that conclusion and we would not want to. But at the same time, given that our relationship with Canada is based on a history of dominance, can we accept that the Charter of Rights and Freedoms is the only way to protect individuals? I am convinced the Charter would not work for us. Do we want to run to Canadian courts every time there is a problem in our communities? How could we afford the time and expense in settling our disputes? Shouldn't our own people and our own values be involved in that process?

A related issue is the role of urban Indians in the governments we create. I don't have the answers for that. All I know is that urban Indians have to be part of the process of finding those answers. To me, the first step in resolving these issues of individual rights and urban people is acceptance by Canada of our peoples' inherent right to govern ourselves. We need to involve urban people, our family members in the cities, in the implementation of self-government. I am not exactly sure what that will mean in the development of institutions of self-government but I do know it is right to be inclusive.

The governments of Canada want us to tell them exactly what our governments will look like before they'll accept us or approve of our rights. They did not apply that standard to themselves when they created their governments. It took years to evolve the form of government now enjoyed in Canada. At the time of Confederation, the British Parliament did not say to John A. Macdonald, "Pre-define your government in precise terms before we will accept it." They requested general terms and parameters. And now, when we want our inherent right recognized, they insist that we "pre-define" it to suit their views of who we should be. We must insist that Canadian governments not impose their political will on our peoples. We have a right to evolve our institutions and governments. We need the flexibility to do that so we can meet the needs of our peoples, not the needs of Canadian governments.

The First Nations do not want the Department of Indian Affairs to have control of negotiations over self-government. Absolutely not. Why? Because they have spent millions of dollars promoting something called community-based self-government without a single agreement. We want to get away from their failures. We want successful agreements to be negotiated politically. The track record of the Department says to us that we should stay away from them because they do not bargain fairly and they do not support our aspirations.

For us it is also very attractive to have an alternative dispute mechanism, a tribunal or some other entity that will be independent of provincial governments, federal governments, Aboriginal governments, independent of all of us. It would monitor, guide and, if necessary, mediate disputes as we proceed in negotiations on implementing self-government. Specialized tribunals would address the concern that these issues be kept out.

Many misconceptions and some fears about the inherent right of self-government flow from misunderstandings of our aspirations for the future. The **inherent** right of self-government is a very simple concept. It means that our right to govern ourselves comes from our peoples, our distinct past, our cultures. It is not something that can be granted to us by any other society or any other governments. It is ours.

It is important, from our perspective, that the inherent right be recognized as a pre-existing right and that it be enforceable. We have chosen to use the political forum to find acceptance for our inherent right of self-government rather than to assert the right directly, with or without Canada's concurrence, although this course of action remains open.

I don't think anyone should operate on the assumption that we lack existing rights to govern ourselves. It is a fact of life; we had governments long before Canada did, and we continue to have governments. We have the right to govern ourselves. It may not be explicitly recognized within Canadian law, although we believe it is only a matter of time until it is accepted by the courts. Efforts have been made to try to eliminate and regulate our rights through the Indian Act. Nonetheless, we as peoples do not believe for a moment that we need the consent of Canada to be self-governing. That is why we use the word "inherent" to describe our rights.

The concept of "inherent" is also important to us for mental health reasons. To feel healthy about our acceptance in Canada, we need to have our history acknowledged. We have a history independent of the nation-state Canada. Some people have suggested that there is a fair amount of guilt on the part of non-Aboriginal Canadians about the treatment of our people. I have seen that guilt. I don't want to use it. We're not here to do that. Guilt is no basis for a future relationship. At the same time, it is quite a powerful force when it is harnessed for changing the socio-economic conditions for our peoples. We recognize that the support that we have across the country is in part genuine and in part based on guilt. We must work with that fact and build a better understanding.

We have been making some steady progress in the last few years, particularly in the Supreme Court of Canada. These gains have given us some hope that if we have to argue the inherent right of self-government in the Supreme Court of Canada there is a good likelihood that the court will recognize that this right exists in law. I believe it is only a matter of time until our rights are broadly accepted.

First Nations peoples in Canada believe our treaties confirm the inherent right of self-government for treaty signatories. We believe, rightfully, that we already have the right of self-government, and that what is missing is the process to exercise that right. What we should be working towards is a process for implementing the inherent right of self-government.

The implementation process we want, as the Assembly of First Nations, is a treaty-making process. We want to continue what has been our historical choice: treaties.

One of the basic goals of our peoples is to preserve our way of life. In that sense, our goals are not even different from those of the French people in the province of Quebec. We are trying to find a way of making our inherent right of self-government part of the legal and political structure of Canada; in other words, to find an acceptance for us in this country.

We feel that we are not being accepted on our terms, that we are being pushed to define our right for Canada's purposes, in a way that is acceptable to Canada, regardless of whether it is acceptable to us. But this struggle is about our way of life. It is about finding powers to preserve our languages, maintain and develop our cultures, and provide for the needs of our peoples and our societies within our own institutions, so we can progress from generation to generation. We must determine our own path.

We have experienced, under the Indian Act, the sheer will of the majority over us. The majority has not been very respectful of our identity or rights. So we are reaching out, once again, to try to alleviate our concerns with the past. We are saying that we need the inherent right in order to maintain our relationship with our lands, waters, resources and the environment as a whole. We are saying to Canadians that we need to determine and control our destiny using our own values and priorities, but realizing that at the same time there are competing interests and divergent ideas about the future of Aboriginal peoples. We must resist the psychology of dominance, yet still build together.

The important realization for us is that we must develop our idea of self-government in order to move away from dominance. Concrete definitions will develop during the next stage, which is the implementation process. That is where the details and linkages with the other governments will become apparent and where the harmonization will take place. To try to achieve detailed definitions at the beginning will not produce agreement—we cannot possibly anticipate the various circumstances of all the Aboriginal peoples.

When people ask us to compromise, we answer, "What do we have left to compromise?" We are not greedy people. We have nothing left to compromise. We are trying to find a way of accessing the rights that our ancestors had and were promised, and the process of negotiations in and of itself is an act of compromise. We know there is not a level playing field when it comes to Aboriginal people sitting down with the Government of Canada or the provinces on the implementation of our rights. We are trying to show some flexibility, but we expect compromise on the other side, too. You have everything; we have nothing. You have the capacity to compromise; we have nothing left to give.

The collective right of self-government is the first step in trying to create a balance in our relationships in Canada. We will need exclusive jurisdiction for some areas. No one should get the impression that we are not talking about sovereignty for our people and lands. We are talking about a sovereign order of government within Canada. We are talking about exclusive jurisdiction for that order, which is a form of sovereignty within the Canadian federation just like the provincial governments are sovereign.

When it comes to relations with our peoples elsewhere, like in the United States, the reality is that we are going to maintain those relations with families and friends, just as we are going to maintain relations with the indigenous peoples in Central and South America and around the world. Canada cannot stop that, and never will. Our ties to the indigenous peoples worldwide are based on sharing a common situation; they are very strong and we cannot be expected to sever them. It remains to be seen where they will lead, but one thing is for sure—we are working toward international standards on indigenous peoples and indigenous rights. We are doing this collectively, as indigenous peoples at the United Nations. I haven't seen Canadian sovereignty dismembered by our efforts to protect our rights internationally or by our efforts in support of others, even though our inherent rights have not yet been explicitly recognized.

We have been told that we must define the inherent right of self-government, but when we put forward our response, the federal government told us that it was unacceptable. After a lot of soul-searching, I do not know how much clearer we can make our position. The inherent right is being advocated for a purpose: to protect our identities, languages, cultures and traditions, and to ensure our integrity as peoples. We seek to preserve a way of life, to use our own institutions of self-government to deal with the social and economic needs of our people, to heal our communities, and to make some progress so we can have vibrant societies. We want to preserve a distinct way of life that has suffered dramatically under Canadian policies of assimilation.

What powers and jurisdictions do we need to accomplish this? The implementation of the inherent right of self-government can mean many different things. The jurisdiction of our governments should at minimum include power over the administration of justice, the economy as it affects our peoples, business development, child welfare and social development, cultural and spiritual development, and so on. If people fear we will create Aboriginal armies, let me tell you that we are not interested in creating armies. We want to meet the needs of our people.

The implementation of the inherent right of self-government will have some restrictions—restrictions we will impose ourselves. This is what needs to be discussed during negotiations, so each First Nation can make its position clear, given its history. It is absurd to say that there will be no limits if Canada recognizes our inherent right. Of course there will be limits. The limits are not just legal; they are practical, too. We have come to certain conclusions about the political reality in Canada. There are certain things that are completely out of the question, such as our own monetary policy or our own currency. But these are decisions that have been made by us because we are looking to a better future and a continued relationship, not independent states with all that entails.

Right now, when it comes to negotiation of self-government, the limits are not on the part of the federal government; the limits are on the part of First Nations. We know about limits. We know what it is going to be like to negotiate the implementation of self-government with people who are not interested in recognizing our rights. We know how it feels when we lack adequate resources to advance our position. We are the ones who are taking the risks in negotiation so we need some fairness too.

Elder Peter O'Chiese has given us some guidance on how we can work towards building a better future for ourselves and reform the larger Canadian society to accommodate a better collective future. He said we have to heal our people and we have to heal a country. These thoughts are different from those that dominate the minds of the people in power in this country; when they talk about re-shaping Canada, they do not always approach their task with a spirit of accommodating the rights of the many different peoples. When the Prime Minister talks about a new Canada or when the premier of Quebec speaks about Quebec's place in it, they do not use words like healing, harmony and sharing. They talk about power, the division of power among themselves, and they do so without considering our involvement or how our grievances can be addressed.

For them, unity is built on a written document that parcels out political power in compartments. For us, unity for Canada must be based on the need to heal our people and to heal this land. How do we do that when we ourselves are not part of the power structure of this country? How do we make fundamental changes so that our place will be respected and our rights will be honoured?

First, we have to agree upon what it is that we seek to change in the other society, what problem we should focus on. Rebuilding ourselves and our societies and renewing our peoples' strength must always be the primary goal of First Nations leaders, because we have experienced great suffering.

A second task is to change the political structure and laws of this land. It is important for us to find a place for our peoples within the political structure and laws of a reformed Canada. We must change the old ideas, which see us as outsiders to the political structure of Canada, and start the healing process. We can begin by targeting concepts like the supremacy of Parliament.

It may make a lot of sense for non-Indians, but when parliamentary supremacy is applied to us—when Canada's political will is imposed on us through its laws—it becomes oppressive. Our voices do not matter; they outnumber us, so they decide what is best for us. We have never agreed to be ruled by a non-Native parliament. We will never subject ourselves to the idea that peoples other than ourselves have the exclusive power to make decisions on who we are, where we live, how we live and what our future holds. The principle of self-determination, which belongs to all members of the human family, belongs to us as well. People must chart their own futures, rather than having them chart-ed singlehandedly by Parliament.

The Indian Act had nothing to do with our wishes or desires. It came from somewhere else, from Parliament, and that is why it has not worked. That is also why the Indian Act and the bureaucracy it bred, the Department of Indian Affairs, are such big impedi-ments to our progress as peoples. Part of our struggle is to change laws like the Indian Act that result in domi-nance over our people. But Parliament is not the only problem for us; another is the courts.

The Gitksan and We`tsue`ten land claim, which was lost in the British Columbia Supreme Court in 1990 but overturned in part recently by the Court of Appeal, shows us another old idea that we must change. It is called the underlying title of the Crown and it pre-sumes that the people who were here first, the First Nations, have inferior rights or no rights in comparison with those who came later. It means our land rights can be wished away by the newcomers at their whim. It pre-sumes that the First Peoples have no pre-existing rights unless the settlers and their institutions decide we have those rights. This idea of the underlying title of the Crown prevents our people from reaching just settlements involving their land claims across this country and breeds other concepts such as the extinguishment of our aboriginal land rights. But how can our relationship to the land be erased? There is something fundamentally wrong with this country if it cannot recognize the pre-existing rights of peoples who were here before these newcomers and settlers. We are willing to share; is Canada?

We also have to work hard to fight another concept, another old idea, that is part of Canadian society. We saw it during the army occupation at Oka, and it is called the rule of law. Government ministers condemned the Mohawk people, and in particular the Warriors of that society, for their acts of defiance. They condemned all Mohawks for the defence of their land. And how did they generate public support for the use of the army against the Mohawk people? They did it by rallying Canadians around the concept of the rule of law, the notion that everyone must obey their laws, even if those laws are unjust. It is a concept imposed on us to support the government's dominance. We have treaty rights and aboriginal rights in Canada, yet when we try to assert these rights to feed ourselves and our families by hunting, fishing or trapping, we are faced with prosecutions under the Canadian rule of law. There is a double standard in the rule of law.

These concepts are not appropriate or just for a state with distinct indigenous peoples who have been excluded from developing or influencing them. We do not embrace them and we have suffered because of them. So our struggle is not only to rebuild our societies, which is very important, but to re-structure Canada, to alter the fundamental thinking of the legal and the political systems of this country. If we fail to accomplish that task, we will have two alternatives. One is to choose to be subjected to the supremacy and dominance of another society. The other is to seek what some people in Quebec are seeking, and that is an independent path. These are our choices: to change Canada, accept the status quo or chart an independent course.

If our voices are resisted or rejected, I can assure you we will not be passive witnesses to this fate. Wardship in Canada is dead; we will and must assert our self-determination. One of the basic points about self-determination is self-representation, and what that means—in very plain language, to borrow a style of the Elder—is this: we speak for ourselves and no one speaks for us. We will not be completely at the whim and mercy of the majority of Parliamentarians who are non-Aboriginal. This dominance will end and we can see clearly our options for ending it. It is a partnership we seek, not continued dominance.

I sometimes wonder at what point we should surrender, at what point we should just withdraw. We compromise and show flexibility with governments but to be asked to always give more ground is to be asked to humiliate ourselves. It is as simple as that. It amounts to surrender. We cannot defend our people against the actions by governments. We do not have the financial or political power to do it. All we have is the right to protest, to show our dissent. From time to time, we also show our anger in order to make governments move towards our way.

What we are looking for is not just power to deal with the social problems we face but reconciliation with Canada. We are trying to find a way of creating harmony in the country. The way you achieve that is to produce justice; our people have to feel justice, not just think about it. We have to experience it before we can believe it. There is absolutely no way that First Nations governments can meet the needs of the First Nations peoples without the help of the provinces or the federal government. What we are asking is to become partners working towards the same future.

# Our Home and Native Land

One of the long-standing conflicts between First Nations and the Canadian government has been over land claims. Almost every First Nations community is located on a reserve, which is a tract of land — usually the size of a postage-stamp — set aside by the federal government for specific bands of Indian people. No one particular Indian person "owns" the land; it is held by the Crown for the collective benefit of everyone in the Indian band. The notion that First Nations lands, which we have occupied since before contact, must now be held by the government on our behalf is both bizarre and insulting. It is like someone coming for dinner uninvited and then taking your house as their own: it's pretty presumptuous, and the sting does not wear off.

There are more than two thousand reserves across Canada for in excess of six hundred Indian bands. These reserves sometimes include parts of a band's traditional territories but in many cases, First Nations have been relocated to new areas either because of the encroachment of non-Aboriginal settlements or because of the destructive impact of economic and resource development. Some treaties, like the Prairie treaties concluded after Confederation, have clauses suggesting that all land rights were extinguished and surrendered to the federal Crown. In exchange for this surrender, land was promised to Indian people, based on a formula of a certain number of acres per family. Many First Nations peoples dispute the suggestion that all lands were surrendered in the treaties and contend that this idea showed up in the written text but was not part of the understanding the treaty signatories had about the relationship. In some cases reserve lands were set aside for Indians after treaties were made. But the actual lands transferred did not fulfill the formulas promised at treaty time. In other cases, lands have been taken from First Nations without compensation, without respect for legal standards and sometimes in an intentionally misleading way.

The Oka crisis was about land claims, so are the ongoing dispute between the Lubicon Lake Crees and the province of Alberta and the struggle between the Innu people of Davis Inlet and the federal government. Most First Nations controversies can be traced to land disputes. Either lands are taken, or else development proceeds on First Nations lands without the consent or permission of First

Nations peoples. Sometimes developments proceed even when lands are subject to claims. The disputes over hydro-electric development, logging, mining and other projects have their origins in conflicts over land. While the exact figures are disputed, it is estimated that First Nations peoples in Canada control less than one percent of the land mass. The Inuit, through land claims, have been more successful in gaining access to land rights in the North.

It was only in 1973 that the Canadian government first truly acknowledged that First Nations peoples do have a legal interest in their land. After an important court case between the Nishga people of British Columbia and the Crown, the government introduced a process to address land disputes. One part of this process is called a Comprehensive Land Claims Policy, which is for those First Nations who have not signed treaties and who have never ceded their lands to the Crown. Only one First Nations community, the Gwich'in in the Northwest Territories, has settled a claim under these provisions since 1973. Then there is the Specific Claims Policy, which is supposed to address grievances stemming from treaty violations and mishandling of reserve lands by the Department of Indian Affairs. Only thirteen of over two hundred specific claims have been settled. Neither of these processes has worked with any measure of success. Some estimate that at the current rate of progress a First Nation wishing to make a Specific Land Claim would face *nearly a two-hundred-year delay in having its dispute resolved. This is likely a modest estimation; the more likely outcome would be what lawyers call "settlement by inertia." In other words, if one party does nothing for long enough the problems will just go away—because the aggrieved will get tired of waiting and the conflict will be moot, in this case the lands will be fully developed by government or industry.*

*In 1991 the federal government set up the Indian Specific Claims Commission to look at specific claims that were allegedly mishandled by the Department of Indian Affairs. Depending how it operates in the future, the Commission may offer some hope. Although it is led by the prominent and respected Indian lawyer Harry LaForme, it has been given a lukewarm reception by First Nations leaders because it cannot hear appeals from land claims disputes and reach a binding decision; it can only review matters and then make recommendations to the Minister of Indian Affairs, who retains absolute discretion on whether to accept or reject them.*

For many years our peoples have been committed to working together on a fair and just resolution of our land disputes. We see this as not only in our best interests as peoples but also in the interests of the nation and all Canadians. We want our outstanding land and resource disputes to be resolved through negotiation, not through litigation or confrontation.

However, we are not making any progress on our land claims because the federal government, as represented by the Minister of Indian Affairs, continues to insist on controlling the entire resolution process on claims. We have consistently called upon the federal government and the Canadian people to establish a totally independent claims resolution process where we can be assured fair treatment. I have been unable to get the government to agree to such a reasonable and just approach.

We are the only peoples in Canada who are consistently treated paternalistically and in a condescending manner by governments and the bureaucracies of government. I hope at some point we will be able to stop focusing on problems with the federal claims policy and discuss, on a more positive note, reports of the successful resolutions of land claims.

Under the current policy, the Canadian government still continues to act as lawyer, judge and jury over claims we bring. No matter how you view the Indian Specific Claims Commission, the new Commissioner only has the power to recommend to government, not to reach settlements of disputes. The real control still resides with federal bureaucrats and ultimately with the Minister of Indian Affairs. The policy of control by the federal government has not changed. The paternalism is still there. The only change is the Commission's capacity to review administrative decisions that have been made against the interests of First Nations by bureaucrats.

The federal government has yet to adequately address its own conflict of interest in relation to claims. The government is, after all, supposed to be the trustee for the best interests of the First Nations. The current policy is not consistent with legal principles Canadian courts have set out on the duties of the Crown not to put itself in a hostile position towards First Nations. All the evidence we have indicates that the goal of the federal policy is to minimize the costs of settlement, to entice or to force already desperate people to sign minimal agreements because they have been waiting for a settlement for so long. It takes positions hostile and antagonistic to our land rights.

In December 1990, the Chiefs Committee on Claims developed a series of recommendations on how land claims policies should be changed. These recommendations reflect a broad consensus and have been ratified by the First Nations in national and regional forums. The recommendations call for a fair process, binding decisions and proper compensation. They reflect the fundamental principles that must be adopted by the Canadian government if an effective claims resolution process is to be put into place. The recommendations call for a claims resolution process that is independent from government—not a partially independent one, not a quasi-independent one, but a fully independent process consistent with recognized principles of law.

Claims policy, in our view, must be flexible enough to deal with the diverse nature of claims and not tailored to fit within the narrow policy and process requirements of the federal bureaucracy. I urge those interested in claims to review the Assembly's position paper on the subject and see first-hand the reasonable approach we have recommended to the Canadian government.

Almost everyone who has examined the issue of land claims has recommended that an independent land claims resolution process be established. Such recommendations have been put forward on many occasions by the Canadian Bar Association, the Canadian Human Rights Commission and by many others, including several prominent church organizations. In fact, the Parliamentary Standing Committee on Aboriginal Affairs put forward this same recommendation as a result of its examination of the Oka crisis. Despite all this, the federal government has refused to make a commitment to an independent land claims resolution process, and instead insists upon maintaining its immense control over the process and is building up the existing bureaucracy under the guise of accelerating the settlement of claims.

We are not fooled by Canada's response to our recommendations.

The Order in Council issued by the Privy Council in 1991 to set up the Indian Specific Claims Commission incorporates a narrow set of criteria from the existing claims policy, further limiting how decisions can be reviewed. We find these terms of reference completely unacceptable for obvious reasons. First, there was no consultation with us. Second, the terms of reference and limitations on compensation are not consistent with legal principles. They violate the concept of equality guaranteed under the Charter of Rights and Freedoms. Third, the terms of reference and limitations on the process represent a serious breach of the federal government's fiduciary obligations to First Nations. Fourth, these limitations tie the hands of the Commission and take away its independence. And finally, the restrictions imposed upon the Commission are inconsistent with then Prime Minister Brian Mulroney's promise that his government is prepared "to go far beyond the status quo."

We know one thing: only the bureaucracy is bene-
fiting from this initiative. Unless there is fundamental
change, the vast majority of outstanding claims will not
be resolved. We only need to look with sadness at the
history of the Alberta Lubicon Cree who have not been
able to move ahead after a twenty-year struggle to support the need for urgent change. A process that is fair
and equitable must be established. Respect for our
inherent aboriginal and treaty rights must guide future
government policy. We know that the people of Canada
support First Nations in our struggle for justice and we
need to move to make the land claims process work.

# Moving Towards Self-Sufficiency

The massive dispossession of First Nations peoples has brought dramatic changes in First Nations economies. Cash economies are replacing traditional sustenance activities, which required a large land base, and welfare and poverty are the hallmarks of First Nations communities. Unemployment is estimated at approximately seventy percent on Indian reserves across the country. The impact this kind of economic distress has on the lives of Indian people is staggering.

Dealing with poverty and economic development is a key issue for First Nations leaders, and Ovide Mercredi's commitment to ending poverty and rebuilding First Nations economies is evident. He is keenly aware of the social and human costs of poverty, especially for children.

While each of the specific areas where First Nations are experiencing problems is significant and needs attention, the *distinct problems are also connected. Problems with the criminal justice system, for example, are related to poverty and racism. And problems with self-esteem and suicide are related to the fact that First Nations peoples are not treated fairly by Canadian society. When you are not considered capable of controlling your own life or community, the result is despair.*

*When six Innu children in Davis Inlet attempted a group suicide in a frozen shack in early 1993, it was a barometer of hopelessness. The enormous pain, despair and victimization suffered by children like these is beyond description. Suicides, attempted suicides, and alcohol and solvent abuse are rampant in that community, primarily because the Innu people of Davis Inlet were forcibly relocated in 1967. This despair is not restricted to Davis Inlet. Suicide rates in Aboriginal communities across the country are the highest in the industrialized world.*

❋ ❋ ❋

It is not easy to be a First Nations person in Canada today. It is even less easy to be a First Nations child in Canada because that almost guarantees that you are living in poverty. Canada has known about our poverty for many years but has done little to address it. Now the world has seen our situation because of the spotlight on Davis Inlet. Our leaders want to do something for our children, to improve their opportunities and living conditions. We struggle for political changes because we want to see their lives improve.

The better life community leaders, parents and teachers in Davis Inlet want for their people involves many things, but the central one is healing. They want to heal their people, and to heal their children. I wish it was as easy as commitment and will. Unfortunately, the decision to change the situation is not entirely theirs to make. The government has to assist in rebuilding the community of Davis Inlet because the government cruelly relocated them in the first place. But we have to make the first move. We need to find a better place for the people of Davis Inlet on the mainland so that they can know a better life than what they have been subjected to since being relocated in 1967.

I want all of our children to have dreams—not bad dreams, but good dreams. Dreams about what they want to become, how they can strengthen each other. The problems that our children are having are not peculiar to Indian people. The problems they face in terms of drinking, abuse and suicide are present in any community where there is lost hope. It is important to see that we have these problems not because we are First Nations peoples—they are not part of our identity—but because we are poor and because we are powerless.

What is the future for the young people of Davis Inlet? What hope do they have? What dreams do they have? They have the same dreams as any other normal children in Canada. They want a future for themselves just like all Canadian children. The only problem for our peoples is that when we dream these dreams we are without control of our land and our governments—and without this control, our economic future is grim. The problems in Davis Inlet are not just problems of being Indian. They are not just problems with drinking or abusing gasoline. They are problems with being poor, being relocated and not having control over their own lives. The fact that we have problems does not mean we have to give up on our dreams. It means we have to try even harder to achieve them.

Many of the changes the people of my generation are seeking are changes that may not be visible until the next generation comes to power, when the young people of today become leaders of our communities. I wish I could make it so they would benefit immediately from the work we are doing. It is painful to know they will have to wait even another day before solutions can be brought to the problems we all have. But we have to get up and keep going. We have to keep believing the people of Canada will not turn a blind eye to our situation. We have to keep working for change with Canadians.

When I was elected National Chief I didn't intend to become the national preacher. But I think it's important to pour out my feelings so people will have an idea what I think, who I am, and how I believe we can work together to heal our people. You see, I am basically an optimist. I know we are in pain. I know we are suffering. I know we have problems, serious social problems like family violence, abuse and suicide. But I also believe that we have the knowledge, the talent and the strength to change our lives for the better. We can do it. But before we get there, we must get rid of some obstacles that stand in the way of our progress, and one of them is that sense of inferiority—the residue from the residential school system, the by-product of political dominance of our people. We have to get rid of it, put it aside for our own sake and for the sake of future generations. It builds barriers between us and makes us think less of each other.

It is no longer acceptable to be just complainers about our social and economic conditions. It is no longer enough just to blame others for our pain and misery. What does it take? How many pennies does it take to stop family violence in our homes? How many dollars does it take to prevent child abuse in our communities? We must begin the healing process for the recovery of our First Nations peoples with whatever resources we have. It must start with us, here in our hearts. Yes, we

will need outside support, but we have to do everything
we can on our own, too.

When I was sixteen—which was not *that* long ago, just
over thirty years—not one single person on our reserve
collected welfare. Our people were self-sufficient and
the wage economy was virtually non-existent. Our fish-
ermen from Grand Rapids went all over to trade their
catch. We were not restricted like we are today by the
Fresh Water Fish Marketing Corporation. The quality of
the fish we traded was tops and the price was good.
Unfortunately, because of hydro-electric development,
the quality of the fish we can catch has gone down and
so has the price. This has been very hard on the community. We were not starving before, and we were not
dependent. Today we see great poverty.

I believe much can be accomplished by rejuvenat-
ing our traditional economies. Given that the vast
majority of our people still earn their living by hunting,
trapping, fishing and gathering, it is worthwhile re-
examining this option. We require sensitive governments, a partnership approach, and an injection of fiscal
resources to revitalize sustenance activities.

The majority of First Nations leaders condemn the
present welfare system as extremely destructive. It hin-
ders the capacities of our people to contribute to the

country and it destroys the hopes and dreams of First Nations youth. How can poor people contribute to the nation when poverty brings ill health and substandard education? We need to find new approaches to a system that dominates the lives of a large proportion of our people. Collective responsibility and careful planning are required. Financial assistance is going to be needed, too. However, when most of the population lives at the subsistence level or is on social assistance, it's not surprising that the quick solutions favoured by the federal government seem most expedient.

Our people have been poor for far too long. Most of our communities suffer with second-class services; some even lack such basic services as sewer and water systems. To break from this experience, First Nations governments must have a secure fiscal base to meet the needs of our people. We need access to our land and resources, and this must be part of the planning for self-government. A new land claims process is required. For greater autonomy, our fiscal authority must be direct; we need to control our own funding. The fiscal arrangements we arrive at must elevate First Nations governments from mere administrators of pre-designed programs. This will encourage responsible government and allow us to be independent and self-reliant, to meet our day-to-day needs and address our social problems.

There is absolutely no justification—none what-
soever, in a wealthy country like Canada—for an estimated four hundred thousand First Nations people to
be unemployed by the year 2000. But that's what is
predicted. We should be making plans right now to
make sure that there are adequate jobs, training and
education, so that our young people will find employment opportunities and economic development opportunities before the year 2000. Yet we are not part of
that economic planning process. We have no support
and we are not engaged in any discussions with governments to plan for a response to this dire economic
future our peoples face. We are not part of annual First
Ministers conferences on the economy. We are excluded even though our poverty is the most extreme in
Canada. This has to change if we are going to progress.
We need to be planning a better economic future and
this can't happen until we meet with Canadian governments.

I do a lot of travelling, and people often ask me how I
can maintain the pace. Quite frankly, I do not know
how I do it. The Elders help me stay strong. I have jour-
neyed around the country visiting our people because I
want to understand who it is that I am representing and
what our collective voice should say. I want to reach out

and give our people an opportunity to tell me what it is that they expect me to do. I want to witness first-hand how our people live across the country.

Last year I went to a reserve near Temiscaming in Northern Quebec, where I spoke to a group of students from grades 3, 4 and 5. I like to meet children because they speak their minds and do not worry what other people think about their views. We were up on a platform and I asked them to give me some direction as their National Chief. I asked them, "What advice would you give me so I can be a more effective leader for the Assembly of First Nations?" I got quite a few responses.

One common suggestion was "Listen to your mother." My mother, Louise, is one of the few people who can get into a car in Grand Rapids, Manitoba, begin a conversation there and end it in Winnipeg, which is a distance of some three hundred miles. So I have listened to her for many years and learned a great deal. I certainly qualify on that score and I will keep listening to the good advice of my mother.

Another young person said to me, "Do your homework." I think that is good advice for anybody who is involved in advocating for the rights of our peoples. Preparation is everything. You wouldn't walk into a room of politicians who are there to discuss your peoples' rights unless you are well prepared to ensure the rights of future generations. I will carry this suggestion with me and do my utmost to respect it.

One other young person in the class must have been watching television when I appeared before the Quebec National Assembly because this young person said to me, "Do not fight." I think that is good advice too, particularly when we are involved in very sensitive work, trying to reform the country in such a way that it does not become dismembered because of bad feelings or hot tempers. It would be very unfortunate if decisions were made because of bad feelings or resentment. That young individual's advice is consistent with what the Elders tell us, and I take it very seriously. The Elders tell us to try to maintain the traditional approach of peaceful co-existence with other Canadians, and that through peace we can deal with problems in a way that will bring meaningful change.

When I visit the city of Toronto, I am struck by the many peoples from different lands, cultures and societies. The voices of multicultural groups in Canada express a common plea for respect, not just for individuals but for collectives. They are seeking greater recognition of and protection for multiculturalism in Canada. For them, true equality will come from respect for them as a collective and on that basis individual rights can enjoy real meaning. The Black community in the city of Toronto feels aggrieved, just as First Nations people in the city of Winnipeg feel aggrieved, about the use of police force. They do not feel aggrieved as individuals, although individual cases have come forward; they feel aggrieved as a group. That grievance cannot be resolved by conducting investigation upon investigation into the treatment of individuals. Their grievance can only be healed by respecting the Black or First Nations communities as collectives and building new relationships where problems exist.

This is what our people are doing in urban centres. They want to end assimilation and the misery of poverty and unemployment. Our people want to change their social and economic conditions in a very practical way, by creating institutions within urban centres to deal with needs like education and child welfare.

The inherent right of self-government that we speak of can have many different faces; it does not have to be uniform in its application. It can mean one thing for the urban population and something quite different for First Nations peoples with a land mass or a territory. The range and the scope of the powers can be different from region to region and even from time to time. Being the practical and the prudent people that we are, we tell Canadian politicians that we are willing to sit down and negotiate the application of self-government.

There is a valid sense of grievance about our treatment in all parts of Canada. Our people have experienced a collective form of societal and economic victimization. Those wounds cannot be healed until we do something to change our experience. The wounds are there in my parents, they are there with me and they will be there with my children. If we maintain the status quo, we perpetuate that system of victimization. The only real opportunity for First Nations peoples to start on the road to recovery is to persuade Canadian people and governments to respect us, not as just individuals but as distinct peoples who are part of the family of the human race.

I do not know the business world. I am from the trapline, even though I later went to law school and learned about that profession. My experiences have been mostly in social development in areas like child welfare, health and education. There is little, in my view, that can be done by individual corporations or by organizations like the Canadian Council for Native Business to help our situation if we do not make structural reforms in the Canadian state. The help provided by business people may benefit a small population in our communities, but the real social and economic recovery can only take place if there is a new relationship with Canada that is based on the right of the First Nations peoples to define their own futures. Business people can help us deal with the poverty in First Nations communities by working with us to create employment and economic development opportunities and to provide training and education. They can also help us with planning. But we have to change governments first so that we can put plans in place for the future.

Recently I went to the Nass Valley, which is the home of the Nishga First Nation. Two hundred years ago they met Captain Vancouver. One hundred years later—just one hundred years after Captain Vancouver was sighted by these people—they had already been put into the position of having to negotiate for the recognition of their land rights. For one hundred years they have been told they have no land rights, no resource rights. It was not until the government of Mike Harcourt agreed to recognize and resolve the Nishga people's land claim that they see an opportunity to control an area of land in their traditional territory that is still rich with natural resources. And if we can succeed in ensuring that the resolution of land disputes includes self-government, then the Nishga people will have an opportunity to deal with their own poverty. But they will still need a partnership with Canadians from the business community—one that respects their own values in terms of the protection of the environment.

For some time our people have been trying to find ways of being more self-sufficient. It is quite apparent to us that in order to reach that objective, we are going to need the help and cooperation of the Canadian people and the corporate or business communities. Unlike some other First Nations leaders, I do not believe in absolute sovereignty or independence for our people, because I think it is impossible to close our minds and our hearts to the experiences of other people in this country. We cannot pretend that we are the only human beings on this planet or that we are totally independent. No society anywhere in the world has absolute sovereignty. We know from experience, in just looking at the world economy, that not a single nation-state is absolutely sovereign in terms of its economic policy or political direction.

We live in an era of interdependence. We have to come to the realization, as First Nations, that we have to lift ourselves up, and in the process reach out to other Canadians and their governments to help us elevate our social and economic conditions. We must eliminate poverty and suffering so that we can contribute to a common vision of economic and social progress for all the individuals that should benefit from sharing our Mother Earth.

I can tell you without any doubt in my mind or heart that the people I represent want to change this country in a fundamental way which can strengthen, not destroy it. We want to be part of the riches of this country, both as sharers and creators of wealth. We want to be part of the social and political life of Canada. But, equally important, we want the right to be different. We want to be able to survive as distinct peoples, to pursue our own dreams as peoples who have been here since time immemorial. We want to reach deep into our past, to secure those values and priorities that are essential for the development of strong societies. We have much to contribute, but we need space to be different in order to belong with Canada.

There are many resources in this country, and Canadians respond to this with massive resource development. We believe people have forgotten the importance of protecting the environment for future generations. The peoples that I represent, those with an indigenous philosophy, have a world view that is different from that of the corporate mainstream. We have a view of the environment that does not stop all forms of development, but allows it to proceed in a way that respects the environment and ensures that it is protected for future generations. Our philosophy of economic development is ingrained in our culture. We have distinct beliefs about how we should relate with the planet, how we should deal with development, and how we should respect the planet itself. It is easy to talk about respect in the context of human beings respecting each other. But to respect Mother Earth as a living entity is not easy, particularly when the preoccupation of economic development may well be to exploit natural resources rather than preserve or sustain them. That endangers our common survival and the survival of future generations who are relying on us to preserve the planet for them.

We have to take some lessons from *Our Common Future*, the Brundtland Report on the state of the environment. This international report says to people around the world that we have to stop and think about what we are doing with this planet. The peoples who can help us are the indigenous peoples of this world. I am not referring to just the First Nations of Canada, but also the First Nations in Central and South America, and the indigenous peoples in New Zealand, Australia and Europe, all of whom who share a common vision regarding our relationship with the land. Our philosophy is not founded on exploitation but on different concepts of resource development, economic renewal and economic development. We believe that relationships do not have to be exploitative.

In Canada, holding down the deficit has become a fixation for government. Think about it. The Prime Minister announces that the economic agenda is to retire the deficit, and that is the economic plan for the future. Why can we not generate wealth in this country that is good for all of Canada? Why can we not deal with the needs of all the people? Why can we not move the economic agenda beyond the deficit and deal with the initiatives and incentives that are necessary to sustain human life, and do it in a way that creates a decent standard of life for all people? We need a standard of life that does not make distinctions based on race, colour or religion, a standard of life that will be available to all human beings in this country.

Why can we not design with the government of Canada an economic strategy to deal with unemployment, to deal with the housing needs of all Canadian people, and most of all to redress the wrongs that have devastated the Indian people, the Métis and the Inuit of this country? To his credit, Brian Mulroney created five thousand Aboriginal businesses because of his government's economic policies. The government says it wants to increase that to ten thousand. This is an important objective. But for us as First Nations peoples,

business development is just one aspect of the progress
we need. These developments often benefit individuals
but not necessarily entire communities. Community
economic development is what we require to really
address our poverty.

I spend a lot of time talking to young First Nations
people in kindergarten, elementary school and high
school. By the year 2010, they will be adults, and many
will be raising their own families. When I look at them
right now, I see the sparkles in their eyes. I remember
that once I too had sparkles in my eyes. I am sure that
my parents had those same sparkles in their eyes when
they were young. For many, those sparkles died, because
there was no hope for change, for economic opportunities, or for that matter for individual advancement. They
grew up knowing only despair. Poverty crushes the spirit.

I do not want to see our young people reach the
age of sixteen, seventeen or eighteen with no economic
prospects, no sense of who they are or what they can
contribute. But the people I represent do not have the
economic power to ensure equal opportunity and a better future on our own. That is why I say that while I
believe in our sovereignty, I do not believe it can or
should be absolute sovereignty. Absolute sovereignty
would mean that we should not expect any relationship
with the federal and provincial governments, with

Canadians, in dealing with our economic needs and our poverty.

The people I speak to, the ones I meet at the community level in my travels, want hope. Their dreams are shattered. They need an opportunity to get away from welfare, to feel good about themselves so they can contribute to their own development as human beings. I have learned a great deal during my time as National Chief. I have listened to the Elders, and I take their advice very seriously. When we began to deal with governments, the advice that we received from Elder Peter O'Chiese was that the objective for the Chiefs was to heal a people, and to heal a country. He said that the way the Chiefs will accomplish this is to find ways to lift each other up. If we do not work together, if we do not lift each other up and find a common understanding, we will always have this social gap between us and the rest of Canada. The people I represent will continue to be victims in their own country, and they do not want that future. My own opinion, based on meeting many Canadians, is that Canadians do not want that future, either.

● ● ●

*Over the past few years there have been many important studies and commissions—including the Royal Commission*

*into the Prosecution of Donald Marshall, Jr., and the
Aboriginal Justice Inquiry of Manitoba, to name a few—
that have indicated that the criminal justice system has failed
for First Nations. While many reports have been issued, the
response of the federal government has been slow and largely
non-supportive of First Nations visions of how to improve
the situation. The movement towards self-sufficiency in
dealing with criminal disputes is a strong one today among
First Nations peoples.*

The mistreatment of First Nations peoples in the
Canadian criminal justice system is nothing short of
tragic. Dealing with this issue is challenging because the
inequities faced by members of First Nations within the
criminal justice system are overwhelming. I want to
consider how we can meet these challenges through
self-government, and how we can create paths for
change for the First Nations peoples.

The injustices experienced by First Nations people
in the Canadian criminal justice system have been so
pervasive that the system has lost the respect and support of both the Canadian public and the First Nations.
First Nations peoples view the criminal justice system
with cynicism; words such as "fairness" and "justice"
have a hollow ring when one confronts the stark reality

of how this institution has impacted our lives. The statistics speak for themselves. In British Columbia and Alberta, Aboriginal people represent five to seven percent of the provincial population, yet constitute thirty to forty percent of admissions to prisons. In Manitoba and Saskatchewan, Aboriginal people represent eight to ten percent of the population but compose forty-six to sixty percent of the prison population. A recent study concluded that a treaty Indian boy turning sixteen had a seventy percent chance of at least one stay in prison by the age of twenty-five. The corresponding figure for a non-Indian was nine percent.

The impact of the justice system on Aboriginal people is starkly exposed in the opening paragraph of the Report of the Aboriginal Justice Inquiry of Manitoba in which the Commissioners write:

> The justice system has failed Manitoba's Aboriginal people on a massive scale. It has been insensitive and inaccessible, and has arrested and imprisoned Aboriginal people in grossly disproportionate numbers. Aboriginal people who are arrested are more likely than non-Aboriginal people to be denied bail, to spend more time in pre-trial detention and spend less time with their lawyers, and if convicted, are more likely to be incarcerated.*

*Commissioners Hamilton and Sinclair. Report on the Aboriginal Justice Inquiry of Manitoba: The Justice System and Aboriginal People, Vol. 1 (Province of Manitoba, 1991), p. 7.

Although this report is specifically directed at
Manitoba, I believe it applies equally to all Canadian
provinces. In total, there have been more than twenty
separate reports on Aboriginal justice issues tabled
across Canada, all of which report the same thing: the
justice system fails Aboriginal people and change is
urgently needed.

The centrepiece of our agenda of self-government
is the ability of First Nations to deal internally with disputes, including those of a criminal nature, according to
our traditional values and laws. Our peoples exercised
our own form of justice for many thousands of years
before we were subject to the Canadian system. Our
form of justice was suppressed by European colonizers
who regarded our forefathers as lawless savages due to a
lack of formal institutional structures and codified laws
in our governments. But lack of codification of our laws
made them no less legitimate than Canadian laws; different does not mean inferior.

Codification was not necessary, as laws were not
understood as a separate intrusive element. Rather, laws
were articulated and understood as general teachings
within the community, in the same way that the teachings concerning hunting and spiritual practices were
part of the larger fabric of life. "Law," therefore, was not
an intrusive element, not separate from one's reality; it

was internal to every citizen. Codification was not required, as laws were understood in the same context as spiritual and moral teachings passed down to future generations through the oral tradition of our peoples.

The dispossession of our societal customs and laws and the imposition of the Canadian justice system with its foreign values was equivalent to cultural genocide. First Nations systems of managing internal disputes and controlling behaviour were replaced by federal and provincial legislation. Many of these traditions may be lost forever. Where they are not yet lost, we must ensure they can be kept alive and have meaning for future generations. We believe that we can deliver a system of justice to our people which is more relevant and more effective than the Canadian system because it focuses upon healing the victim as well as the offender and restoring balance and harmony to the entire community. This is our basic challenge: healing.

The establishment of tribal courts is the closest we can come to a guarantee of our cultural distinctiveness and survival. Our traditions and culture will survive through exercise and implementation. For example, in the area of child welfare, we would rely upon traditional concepts such as the extended family in our decisions regarding placement of a child. In criminal law, decisions would be rendered from the perspective of healing,

compensation and reconciliation as opposed to the
Euro-Canadian values of punishment, deterrence and
imprisonment.

In the event that members of the Canadian justice
community view our position as radical, be assured that
the concept of tribal courts is not new. American tribes
have exercised jurisdiction and administered tribal
courts on their reservations for more than a century.
The challenge to the Canadian legal system is to recognize that the justice system it has designed is neither
infallible nor sacrosanct. It does not always work for
them, and it doesn't work for us. All my people seek is
the opportunity and capacity to exercise our inherent
rights of self-government and justice within our territories. For us, that is justice.

# First Nations and Quebec

Relations between the Quebec government and the ten distinct First Nations who live in that province, the Abenaki, Algonquin, Atikamekw, Cree, Huron, Mikmaq, Mohawk, Montagnais, Naskapi and Malecite, have ranged from stormy to downright hostile in recent years. Three key issues illustrate some of the more prominent strains. First, the ongoing push for a new phase of hydro-electric projects in Northern Quebec, which has been vocally opposed by the Crees. Second, the role of the Quebec police in the Oka crisis and in policing Mohawk communities generally. And third, the clash of Quebec's aspirations for greater autonomy within Canada and for sovereignty or independence with the aspirations of First Nations for self-government.

It is difficult to say if relations with Quebec are that much different from those with other provinces. And the usefulness of that kind of comparison is doubtful; if Quebec is shown to be doing no worse than anyone else, that only serves to emphasize the seriousness of problems elsewhere. But of all the hot spots across Canada, the potential for more confrontation seems most real in Quebec. The National Chief has taken an interest in relations between First Nations and Quebec because of his concern for the situation in that province and also at the request of First Nations in that province. His interest in the Cree situation is informed by the effects of hydro-electric development he has witnessed in his home community in Manitoba.

Ovide has also been committed to developing alliances with French Canadians because of the shared desire to protect languages and cultures from the forces of assimilation. Quebecers seem to have shown a special interest in Ovide Mercredi, perhaps because of his French name and the marriage of a French man into his father's family, or perhaps because he voices frustrations not unlike their own but directed at themselves. Media reaction to Ovide in Quebec has not been especially warm. This has been a disappointment to him. I can remember how shocked he was after appearing before the Quebec National Assembly's Committee To Examine Matters Relating to Sovereignty. He believed there would be a natural alliance between Quebec and First Nations because both are struggling for the recognition of collective rights, but the response was downright hostile. In fact, just getting into the

Committee's meeting room was a battle. There were Montagnais Elders in our delegation who had brought with them a drum, as was their custom, and they wanted to sing a song about their people to open our presentation. The security guards at the National Assembly who conducted a thorough search of everyone would not allow the drum into the room. Ovide would not accept this and said he would not appear before the Committee if First Nations customs and traditions were unwelcome there. After much diplomatic haggling the Committee relented. Still, the Chair, Guy Bélanger, made it clear that he was not pleased about the presence of the Elders or the drum. After their song he chastised Ovide and the delegation for just wanting to put on a show beating the "tom-tom." Needless to say, this did not go over well with the delegation and relations went downhill from there.

First Nations and Quebecers have been pitted against each other over another touchy issue, the use of the word "distinct" to describe Quebec society and First Nations peoples. Many people think Quebec has the market cornered, so to speak, on the phrase "distinct society" and that even using the expression "distinct peoples" in reference to the First Nations is unacceptable. The First Nations see this as a double standard and Ovide refuses to refrain from using it. This has led to a lot of debate over the relationship between Quebec and First Nations. Since the Charlottetown Accord referendum, the distinct society debate has *disappeared, maybe for good, perhaps only for a time. But the relations between First Nations and the Province of Quebec remain delicate.*

●●●

The First Nations are not adversaries of French Canadian interests—on the contrary, we are committed to the recognition of collective rights for all, and this includes the collective rights of French Canadians, both inside and outside Quebec. However, we bring some basic principles and values to this process that cannot be compromised.

Our country has been built upon a distortion of history. It is premised on the idea that there are only two founding nations, the French and the English. Some French Canadians believe this distortion creates the image of only one founding nation, the English. This explains why proposals for distinct society status for Quebec have come forward. In 1867 and in 1982, the First Nations were ignored and a distorted view of Canada was enshrined in our laws. This was done despite our treaties with the Crown and without regard for our lands, resources and rights of self-determination. We were not asked to join Canada, we were simply declared wards of the federal government. This distortion has caused First Nations peoples across Canada great suffering. Our determination for our collective rights and our uncompromising insistence on respect for our peoples are part of an endeavour to liberate ourselves from this suffering.

Our cultures, languages, governments and spirituality have been and continue to be ignored and rejected and sometimes even despised in Canada. We have not been able to adequately promote our identity, rights or values because our authority to do so has been attacked by the Canadian government and laws. We have been forced to fit into a distorted view of Canada that consists of only French and English founding peoples. This is historical denial and the cost to us and to our communities has been enormous.

We are saddened by the fact that Canadians have an image of us that is tainted by this distortion. Canadians know little about our history or circumstances, who we are or what we believe about this country. Some may think we have nothing to contribute to the national political identity. But we are not inferior peoples. We will speak out for our interests. We are peoples with our own histories, languages, cultures and spirituality that we are committed to strengthening and passing along to the future generations who will walk on this Canada, our homeland. Our goals are not selfish. Our goals are about cultural survival. Our goals are about human survival. We have a responsibility for this land, our Mother, given to us by the Creator. That is why our people want to be co-architects in the reshaping of Canada, in transforming our country to a land of opportunity for all peoples but also a land that respects the Earth.

When we look at Canadian laws and government, we see no recognition or acknowledgment of who we are. Our languages, cultures, traditions, governments and spirituality are excluded. It is as if we have been erased from the history books. We have to fight in the courts and practically with our lives to have even the most basic aboriginal and treaty rights respected and implemented by the Canadian state. We have to fight racism and oppression at every turn to protect our identity even though this country is our homeland. We know what it is like to have our collective rights denied, to be strangers in our own land.

We support the struggle by French Canadians for collective linguistic and cultural rights. However, aboriginal and treaty rights must not take a back seat to the collective rights of our French sisters and brothers in Quebec. We cannot build a new Canada, a fully democratic Canada, if First Nations rights are excluded in the pursuit of French and English Canadian rights.

Cultural diversity is a basic principle for our peoples. We accept the worth and dignity of all peoples and cultures without demanding conformity. We have long histories of building alliances amongst ourselves and also with others, based on respecting diversity but working together. Even though they have never been respected by Canada, they demonstrate our ability to build bridges.

Peoples have the right to be different. We don't have to be afraid of diversity. Understanding, unity and cooperation can be achieved by respecting each other's right to be different. Dissention and conflict occur only when one group tries to dominate. It does not have to work this way. We want to build alliances, not hierarchies; we want to end cultural dominance, not maintain it.

Outside of Quebec, First Nations peoples are concerned about the distinct society proposal because of what is missing for the First Nations. What about protection for our languages, cultures, traditions and spirituality? Any national reforms must include provisions that recognize our authority to promote and preserve our identities, rights and values. Let me tell you how urgent this recognition is for our peoples. Of the fifty-three Aboriginal languages in Canada, only three—Cree, Ojibwa and Inuktitut—have a healthy chance of surviving the turn of the century. Why? Because we have no authority to promote and preserve our languages. Our languages have never been respected by the Canadian state. Our people were abused for speaking their languages in the educational system we were forced into. Our Elders tell us that when our languages are lost, our identity is gone. We cannot accept this future. Our languages are in a desperate state. If we lose them, there will be nowhere to go to learn them. We cannot go back to the "mother country" to learn our language—this is our mother country.

These words are not to be construed by anyone as our opposition to the rights of others. We believe that respect for our rights is not advanced by trampling on the rights of others. One of our guiding principles is inclusion. This means that when we deal with constitutional issues like the identity, rights and values of distinct peoples, all collective rights must be embraced in a way that does not create hierarchies or dominance.

I know that the First Nations in Quebec must live with many fears in these uncertain political times. The threat of secession, not to mention the great hostility that has recently been expressed towards us, are all grave issues. To date, the position of the First Nations in Quebec has not been adequately addressed by Quebec or Canada.

The Bélanger-Campeau Commission excluded First Nations when they considered the future of the

Province of Quebec. The Allaire report did the same. They treated our peoples as another government obligation to be tossed around from the federal government to the provincial government. The recent federal Beaudoin-Dobbie Report said nothing of the difficult situation we face. It is as though we are being erased from the very discussions that affect our future so directly.

There is a gap in Quebec between the government and the Aboriginal peoples. I hear it in the words of Cree leaders and the words of Premier Bourassa. The gap needs to be closed and this can only be accomplished by generating understanding. And we cannot do it in a way where we become confrontational, where we become so caught up with ourselves that we deal with the issues purely on an emotional basis and forget about who we are as peoples. We are distinct. We are peoples, we are not just minority populations. The Cree are not just a minority of twelve thousand Quebecers. They are a people, the Cree people, with collective rights to lands, resources, institutions of government, language and culture, to name a few.

It should not take anyone by surprise when we say we are distinct peoples. What was Meech Lake about? How many appearances did we make as the Assembly of First Nations to parliamentary committees set up to review the Meech Lake Accord? Across the country, the First Nations leaders made numerous submissions arguing that we are distinct peoples too, that we also constitute distinct societies. The whole issue raised when Elijah Harper said no to Meech Lake was that the Accord did not respect our identity, it did not respect our distinctiveness within Canada, and it proceeded along this merry road of duality, this road that says to our people: you are not part of Canada because Canada is made up of two founding nations. You will recall that Chiefs across this country pleaded to be included in the Meech Lake Accord, but we were told then that it was a seamless web, that it could not be changed. Had our issues been dealt with then, we would not have seen the defeat of the Meech Lake Accord and we would not find ourselves in the position we are in now with the Province of Quebec.

When we compare our situation with that of the people of Quebec, we know and we accept the fact that they too are distinct people. They also have collective rights to government, the French language and culture. So why does it seem so difficult, when we have this in common, for Quebecers to accept that we too have collective rights of self-determination? I will tell you why. There are myths in this country that must be challenged and put aside. One of these is the idea that Canada is made up of only two founding nations: the English and the French. Quebec has a premier who believes this myth. But we don't fit that perception of reality, so we have to teach the premier. We have to convince him that the world is broader than a vision of the two founding nations. If we are to build a country that is truly democratic and just, it has to incorporate who we are as distinct peoples. It has to reach out to the first peoples. We are often asked not to say "distinct society" because it offends some people in Quebec. I am sorry that some people feel offended by our choice of words, but the concept of distinct society for us is as real as it is for you. No one owns the word "distinct." Why engage in an exclusionary approach to the recognition of what Canada really is?

There have been and will continue to be great debates among our peoples, particularly in Quebec, about the future of Canada. A lot of the debate will focus on the particular future of the Crees in northern Quebec. If we do not become a central part of the discussions now, the myth will prevail; politicians will resolve issues regarding the future of Quebec and the future of Canada and they will divorce the First Nations from the new reality that they make for themselves. This is precisely why we must be determined to maintain First Nations solidarity, so that we can work in

unison to protect our rights, wherever we may live, and
come forward with a strong collective voice to ensure
we are not excluded.

The success of Canada as a nation depends on how
Canadians treat us now, how they address the mistakes
of the past. Our vision of ourselves has been constant, it
has never wavered, not even in our weakest moments in
our history where we fell down. Our vision is to remain
as distinct peoples in our lands. I want to see our rights
and our history so warmly embraced that all the schools
in the country, all the centres of education, will teach a
new political reality and not the myth of only two
founding nations. We can break down barriers and
destroy prejudice. We must create an understanding in
order to eliminate the racism that flows from ignorance
and ensure that our peoples are treated with greater
respect. We cannot achieve this without solidarity, and
we cannot achieve it if we allow ourselves to get
dragged into needless conversations or debates based on
personalities or emotionalism. And we cannot accomplish our objectives by being weak. We have to remain
strong and act on that strength. We have to be able to
face the Canadian people, and in particular, their governments, to demand they take our situation seriously.

But most politicians we deal with are from the old
school. They have other things on their minds that

prevent them from respecting us as distinct peoples. They believe, for example, that sovereignty means only their type of government; that sovereignty cannot include Aboriginal governments. And they are influenced by their own concepts, like parliamentary supremacy, which says that governments are supreme over all individuals and over groups.

The Cree people in Northern Quebec are struggling to prevent the next phase of hydro-electric development of their lands. The small community of Grand Rapids where I come from was devastated by Manitoba Hydro's development project. I know what it means to resist hydro development and I know what happens when you are doomed, because from 1965 to the present, my community has been negotiating a final settlement to compensate us for damages caused by flooding. I know it is important to oppose these developments now and not to wait for later. Later means that they will have dammed the river, destroyed the fishery, destroyed the trapping industry, destroyed the animals.

The perception of our people as having a separate identity, a distinct identity, is nothing new. It is an historical fact. It is a legal fact in the history of Canada. Our treaties are evidence that we regard ourselves as distinct peoples and we have been so regarded by the Canadian nation-state. For that matter, we continue to enter into treaties on a nation-to-nation basis with the Crown. We want to retain that kind of relationship, not as subordinate peoples, but as peoples with our own nationhood, peoples who have the right of self-determination and who can decide for ourselves the nature of our relationships with the various governments of Canada. We will do so on the basis of consent, which is a basic element in relationships between peoples when they respect each other as equals. One does not dominate or impose.

Neither the Quebec government nor the Parti Québecois has yet come to terms with aboriginal self-determination. But there can be no legitimate self-determination or secession by any people in Quebec if the rights of self-determination of First Nations are denied, suppressed or ignored in order to achieve independence. We will not allow the homelands of First Nations in Quebec to be annexed or claimed by anyone without our full and free consent.

The languages, cultures and societies of First Nations in Quebec and Canada are endangered as a result of oppressive federal and provincial policies. We have been, and continue to be, colonized. However, we will not continue to have our cultural and linguistic identities subject to French or English control. Oppression, whether it is inflicted in French or English, is oppression. Domination, whether it is imposed in French or English, is domination.

In certain quarters, including Quebec, our inherent right of self-determination is still being opposed. This is an appalling reflection of harmful, insensitive and assimilative policies. It thinly conceals a stubborn unwillingness to relinquish assumed federal and provincial powers that are unjustifiably exerted over our peoples and territories. Our colonial subordination is an international disgrace for Canada and Quebec. Under international law, both the Charter of the United Nations and the International Bill of Rights recognize: "All people have the right of self-determination. By virtue of that right they freely determine their political status and freely pursue their economic, social and cultural development."

Are the people of Quebec a "people" in the international legal sense? The population of Quebec is made up of a wide range of racial and ethnic groups. It cannot be considered to be a single people with the right of self-determination. Otherwise, the people of Canada would also be a people for the purposes of international law. These interpretations would defeat the essential purposes of self-determination.

Many French Quebecers appear to base their political dreams and aspirations on the right of self-determination. Indeed, it seems to be the foundation for the presumption that an independent state can be formed. I would like some clarification of the basis of Quebec's claim to full sovereignty. Is it self-determination? If so, it has interchangeably been said that "Quebec," "Québecois," "Quebecers," "Quebec men and women" and "the people of Quebec" have the right of self-determination. On more rare occasions, it has also been declared that French Canadians have the right of self-determination. Quebec jurists such as Professor Jacques Brossard insist that it is clearly the French-Canadian nation that has the right of self-determination.

It would appear that the French-Canadian nation centred in Quebec may be a people with the right of self-determination. It is up to French Canadians to make their own case. However, if such a right exists, it cannot be exercised in a manner that denies or impinges on the right of self-determination of First Nations peoples. As jurists from Quebec and elsewhere have suggested, it is uncertain under international law whether this right of the French Canadian nation would automatically include a right to unilaterally secede from the Canadian federation. It certainly does not include a right to trample upon the rights of First Nations peoples.

Even if the French-Canadian nation can achieve independence, it is far from clear what territory an independent Quebec could claim. Some Quebec politicians and jurists have argued that in the case of secession, even if unilateral, Quebec's current provincial boundaries would remain intact. However, Quebec is not a monolith. It is not the home of a single people or culture. In reality, it is the ancestral or historical territory of ten distinct First Nations, the territories of which cover most of the province's land. First Nations territories transcend the geographical limits of the province. They extend into offshore areas, into other parts of Canada and even into the United States. In this context, use of Quebec's geographical borders for self-determination issues makes little sense.

We do not claim that the whole of these traditional territories are the sole and exclusive domain of First Nations. Our heritage in Canada has been, and continues to be, one of sharing our lands and resources. However, the issue of territories and boundaries is complex. It would be dishonest and inequitable to presume that the present boundaries of the province would automatically be those of a sovereign new state. The province of Quebec is defined by an administrative boundary for purposes internal to the Canadian federation. It is not a boundary that reflects the rightful territory of the

French-Canadian nation. In 1898 and 1912, the boundaries of the province of Quebec were extended by political acts of federalism unjustly carried out without the
knowledge and consent of the First Nations whose territories were directly affected. Quebec cannot claim our
lands, handed over for provincial purposes in 1898 and
1912, without our consent.

It is claimed by the Quebec government that First
Nations (both in and outside Quebec) who were not
parties to the James Bay and Northern Quebec
Agreement and the subsequent agreement signed by the
Naskapi Nation had their fundamental rights to land
extinguished unilaterally by federal legislation. This
wholesale breach of human rights was carried out upon
the strict and express insistence of the Quebec government. On the basis of such heinous actions, some
Quebec political leaders claim that First Nations peoples in the northernmost two-thirds of Quebec no
longer have territorial rights on which to base a right of
self-determination. First Nations do not accept such
alleged extinguishment of our rights.

More importantly, no federal or provincial law or
agreement will ever separate us from our homelands,
resources and environment. We have used and occupied
our lands for centuries and we are not about to leave. No
change in a political system can serve as a justification

for severing First Nations peoples from our ancestral ties to Mother Earth. Our relationship to our territories is, above all, spiritual. It nurtures both our identities and our communities in profound ways. No action or secessionist movement can change our relationship with our lands. As former United States President Woodrow Wilson declared in 1917: "No right exists anywhere to hand peoples about from sovereignty to sovereignty as if they were property." It is not up to Canada or Quebec to assume sovereignty over us. The First Nations are not the property of either Canada or Quebec.

Quebec must act honourably in its dealings with First Nations and not act as an adversary. The legal principle of territorial integrity put forth by Quebec is an affront to First Nations. It allows Quebec to create a new legal fiction—wrapping a kind of cloak of legitimacy around claims to our lands. We oppose this fiction. Would sovereignists be willing to recognize, as a paramount principle, the territorial integrity of Canada?

Quebec may hold a referendum on secession to allow Quebecers to decide their future. However, it is not clear to us to whom the term "Quebecers" refers. Does it imply that people of all racial, national and ethnic origins living within Quebec are a single people? Are the French, English, Italians, Greeks, Haitians, Irish, Germans, Jews, Arabs and other ethnic groups

living in the province all one people with the right of
self-determination? Are French Quebecers and First
Nations within Quebec part of a single people? This
view is contrary to ours, which is based on self-determination and self-identification. As Judge Dillard of the
International Court of Justice declared in the Western
Sahara case, "It is for the people to determine the destiny of the territory and not the territory the destiny of
the people."

In the absence of First Nations participation and
consent, the law can only affect the particular territory
that French Canadians can rightfully claim in aspiring
towards independence. In this way, the right of First
Nations to determine the future of our territories
would be recognized and respected. The basis of any
future relationship lies in respect for our right of self-
determination.

Our position is clear. First, it is essential that all
policies and actions of the Quebec government and
National Assembly be consistent with the essential
principle of equal rights and self-determination of peoples contained in the Charter of the United Nations
and numerous other international instruments. Second,
the integrity of Aboriginal territories must be adequately safeguarded and respected. No acts of self-determination by French Canadians centred in Quebec must be

allowed to infringe upon our own collective right of a similar nature. Third, there can be no referendum on Quebec independence without first resolving First Nations issues. Should a referendum on the accession of Quebec to a full sovereignty take place, it must in no way affect First Nations homelands without our free and informed consent.

We have always acknowledged and respected the collective rights of French Canadians. French Canadians in Quebec are a distinct society. However, in the wake of broader objectives that impact severely on the destiny and territories of First Nations, we will not become passive or subordinate societies. We should be building a new partnership based on mutual respect and support for our respective rights. Only through openness of mind and heart can questions of such vital importance to our respective peoples be reconciled. The alternative, which we do not favour, is confrontation.

# The International Lobby

First Nations peoples from Canada are active in international diplomatic efforts to persuade the United Nations and other international bodies to recognize the rights of indigenous peoples in Canada and around the world. This is not a new phenomenon, although the issues are being taken more seriously today because of the growing strength of the international indigenous peoples' movement. In fact, 1993 is the United Nations Year of Indigenous Peoples. This is a culmination of a remarkable feat of lobbying in which First Nations representatives from Canada were instrumental.

Chiefs from Canada have been petitioning the United Nations since before the U.N. was even formally established. During the League of Nations era, before the Second World War, Iroquois Chiefs led by Deskaheh travelled to Geneva to press for attention to the situation of their people. *The Iroquois also travelled to San Francisco in June 1945 in order to attend the conference that led to the formation of the United Nations. Deskaheh was not allowed to attend the conference even after he submitted a petition specifically requesting his entry as a representative of the Six Nations Iroquois Confederacy.*

*First Nations diplomacy has rich historic roots. In some cases, as with the Iroquois, a person is assigned to be the international lobbyist and diplomat. The Iroquois Confederacy even issues its own passports for its delegation and these have been honoured by several European nations, including Switzerland and France. The diplomacy seen today at the international level is a specific extension of the many diplomatic exchanges that First Nations had with each other long before the creation of Canada. For example, cooperation among First Nations led to the development of the Iroquois Confederacy itself—an alliance of six individual nations.*

*Since the Second World War, First Nations leaders have regularly sought the support of international bodies and agencies in the struggle to have human rights respected by Canada. The international presence is driven by the failure of Canadian governments and courts to sensitively address First Nations concerns. Given that Canada prides itself on its international human rights commitments, raising issues at the international level has been an important way for us to* gain attention for our grievances. During the Oka crisis, the United Nations Commission on Human Rights asked Canada for reports on the situation because of its concern for the Mohawk peoples security. The Canadian government had to describe the horrible deterioration in relations and answer embarrassing questions about the safety and welfare of Mohawks behind the barricades who were not getting food.

First Nations representatives have brought before the United Nations Human Rights Committee many complaints about Canada's alleged non-fulfillment of its international human rights obligations. In 1981 the Committee found that Canada had violated the rights of a Maliseet woman from the Tobique Reserve in New Brunswick because it had denied her the right to Indian status and the right to live in her community with her people. Sandra Lovelace was in the same situation as Ovide's mother: she married a non-Indian man and was stripped of her Indian status by the Department of Indian Affairs because of the rules in the Indian Act. After her marriage ended, she wanted to move back home to the Tobique Reserve so she would be nearer her family and her community, and so her children would be exposed to the Maliseet language and culture. But because she was not registered as an Indian she could not get housing on the reserve. She complained to the United Nations that Canada was denying her the right to practise her language

*and culture with her people. The United Nations Human
Rights Committee agreed, and she regained her status after
the 1985 amendments to the Indian Act.*

*First Nations representatives are also active in the
United Nations Working Group on Indigenous Populations
which has been meeting in Geneva, Switzerland each
summer for the past decade (with the exception of 1986,
when budgetary restrictions cancelled the meeting). Some
First Nations organizations in Canada, like the Grand
Council of the Crees, the Mikmaq and the Four Directions
Council from Alberta enjoy special United Nations
consultative status. They have access to meetings and are
recognized as competent to address various human rights
forums in the United Nations and elsewhere. This enabled
the representatives of indigenous peoples' organizations with
consultative status to advocate for indigenous rights at the
1993 World Conference on Human Rights in Vienna.*

*The international First Nations lobby has focused on a
few specific objectives: the formation of an Indigenous
Commission within the United Nations; international
attention to and support for First Nations peoples in Canada
and elsewhere; the development of international standards
for the protection of indigenous peoples' rights; networking
with indigenous peoples from around the world to share
strategies and methods for advancing indigenous claims in
Canada and elsewhere; and the involvement of international*

*observers and human rights experts in the study and monitoring of specific problems or situations for indigenous peoples. On this last point, a special report on treaties is under way, and First Nations from Canada have taken an active interest in it, given the extensive problems with treaties in Canada.*

●●●

The international indigenous community shares a common destiny, and whether our roots are in the Caribbean, the United States, Central or South America, the Philippines, Norway, Greenland, Easter Island or any other part of the world, we must see ourselves as relatives. The people who colonized our indigenous nations are discovering that our liberation from colonization is our common bond and unity. That might be frightening to some but it is not meant to be threatening in any way. A commitment to ending colonialism is a peaceful and just basis for unity and friendship among our peoples.

Throughout the world, particularly in Spain, Italy and the United States of America, 1992 brought many celebrations to commemorate the arrival of Christopher Columbus in the Americas. For us as indigenous peoples, these celebrations were manifestations of the continued rejection and exclusion of our inherent and distinct collective rights as the original peoples of the Americas. The term "discovery" as used in the historical context of the Americas implies dominance and one-sidedness—that the Europeans found us, that we were lost here in our own homeland, as if we were nothing more than wild animals or beasts to be dominated. We have all been exposed to the distorted and unbalanced history that is premised upon the denial of our human dignity. The price for us has been enormous. We have had to endure the silence of our languages and the banning of our traditions and customs. The First Nations of Canada did not rejoice or celebrate 1992, but neither did we mourn. Instead we draw strength from our pride and spirit, and from the truth of our survival in the face of a five-hundred-year history marked by wars, disease, dispossession of homelands and government policies aimed at cultural and physical genocide. The fact that we pull together in international gatherings is a testament to the power and tenacity of our indigenous cultures and civilizations, and to the power of the human spirit in our peoples.

Historians have long debated the population of the Americas prior to the arrival of Columbus. It is now believed that our forebears numbered between 90 million and 112 million persons. Our populations are today a mere fraction of our original numbers due mainly to lack of immunity to the diseases brought from Europe.

The European nations arrived in our lands with a belief in manifest destiny and a strong conviction that they were racially superior. Our peoples were dispossessed of our territories, our self-determination and our inherent rights to language and culture. Even our religious beliefs were deemed inferior and subjected to cultural imperialism. Yet indigenous peoples persevered and still survive as distinct peoples throughout the world. We have our ancestors to thank because they kept alive our religions, languages, governments and cultures even when these were deemed uncivilized, inferior and illegal by the newcomers.

This determination to survive in new situations is captured by the eloquence and words of Chief Poundmaker, who was a political prisoner for some time because of his commitment to the rights of his peoples. Upon his release from prison he said that although the old ways of life on the Prairies were disappearing, it did not mean the Cree Nation should sit back and allow its culture to be destroyed. He knew that our values and way of life could survive.

We have learned the bitter lesson that our rights have been repeatedly violated. We know that our future survival depends on our present abilities to secure not only our lands, but also the recognition of our inherent right of self-rule. The frustration of our efforts to achieve these goals domestically and break free from the chains of colonialism in Canada is the catalyst for the Assembly of First Nations to unite with indigenous peoples from around the world in our shared struggle for self-determination, for land and for human survival.

The indigenous peoples of the world seek nothing more than our collective rights and freedoms and the right to be who we are without being chastised, penalized or exploited. We want to be respected and treated with the same dignity afforded to all human individuals and peoples. We seek respect for the equality of individuals and for the equality of distinct peoples. We want to see and feel justice in the exercise and enjoyment of our human rights—rights that are recognized by the United Nations as the foundation of freedom, justice and peace in the world.

The collective voice of indigenous people has been heard most strongly recently in the United Nations Working Group on Indigenous Peoples, which was established in 1982. This working group is the focal point of international action on behalf of indigenous people and their causes, and has emerged as one of the largest United Nations forums in the area of the advancement of human rights. We hope these efforts will lead ultimately to an international convention on the rights of indigenous peoples throughout this planet.

Our vision of individual and collective rights will be our contribution to the development of human rights and freedoms, since we share a perspective that the world has yet to embrace. The treatment of indigenous peoples mirrors the soul of humanity, and our treatment by the colonizing nation-states is a barometer of the fate of human rights as we move into the 21st century. The world is nearing the brink of ecological destruction, propelled by the same materialistic forces that allowed the colonial powers to view the indigenous people and their lands as objects for exploitation. We have to change the larger society's views of its material needs, especially when these seem to be at the expense of our lands and resources and our ways of life. Our peoples' teachings of harmony and balance with nature must be adopted if humanity is to expand beyond its current destructive thinking and survive the environmental crisis. As Chief Seattle told us many years ago, "The Earth does not belong to man; man belongs to the Earth. This we know: all things are connected, like the blood that unites one family. Whatever befalls the Earth befalls the sons of the Earth. Man did not weave the web of life. He is merely a strand in it, and whatever he does to the web, he does to himself." How true are these words from a great visionary leader of our people.

Indigenous nations know all too well that industrial nations around the world must restructure their thinking and economies to live in greater harmony with the web of life. The unity we are building among indigenous peoples of the Americas is a powerful symbol of the revitalization of our nations. However, we are not alone. Today, in all sectors of human society, we find fellow human beings who share the human spirit for peace, justice and equality between peoples. Ultimately, these beliefs and convictions will help us find support and respect for our peoples and our distinct collective rights. The ultimate vision for us must involve the children of our ancestors and the children of the colonizers joining hands in strengthening the human spirit. The goal we must all aim for is unity, not just with each other but with those who do not yet understand our peoples and our commitment to peace and friendship.

I want to make it very clear that the progress we have made has not been a case of manna falling from heaven. Reform and justice in Canada must overcome a tide of resistance to our collective rights as indigenous peoples. While there have been some substantial developments in Canada that could result in great improvements in the social, economic and political conditions affecting our peoples, like the recognition of our inherent right of

self-government, the fact remains that there still is a
strong potential for failure. In some ways, the progress
we make in Canada could be a model for other nations.

I think it is fair to say that what we are trying to do
in Canada is to end the dominance of one society over
another. There are many ways of describing this process.
Some people use the language of liberation, the language of freedom, the language of justice, or even the
language of reconciliation. But to put it in its proper
context, what we are involved in with Canada is the
struggle for self-responsibility and self-rule. The dominance that has come into our lives in the past hundred
years has not always been there. But the creation of a
nation-state called Canada was by far the most important political event in our lives; it marked the beginning
of the exclusion and rejection of our people and our
rights.

What we have experienced in the past several centuries is the result of one society's assumed superiority
over the affairs and lives of our peoples. That has not
always been the case, because at one point in our history with European nations, the mother countries did
everything in their power to secure the alliance of each
indigenous nation. European nations sought our friendship and alliance. When these efforts met with success,
treaties of alliance and neutrality or treaties of friendship

were made. The European nations regarded us as independent and distinct peoples. So what has changed, and why has this change taken place to the detriment of the First Nations in our country?

The first and most important injustice was the creation of Canada as a nation without our consent. Since that event many things have been done in the name of law. But the laws of Canada exclude the full enjoyment of collective rights by the First Nations peoples. The nation-state has, with a knowing mind and heart, justified the dispossession of the lands of our peoples. It has attempted to destroy our languages and cultures and undermined our collective rights to govern ourselves, all in the name of a so-called free and democratic country. So I will not congratulate the Canadian government for its charity towards us. And I do not intend to thank the provincial governments in Canada should they decide to finally recognize our collective rights. I will say instead, on behalf of the people I represent, it is about time; for it is indeed about time that the collective rights of indigenous people are recognized. It is only just, it is only fair, and it is only one-hundred and twenty-five years in the making.

There are fewer than one million First Nations people in Canada today, and about two million Aboriginal people (including Inuit and Métis), but that was not always the case. Some literature estimates the pre-invasion population of North America at about seventeen million. Today, the Indian population in the United States and Canada combined numbers only approximately four million peoples. Within the world there are approximately two hundred and fifty million indigenous peoples living in seventy countries. This is four percent of the world's population. Most are involved in liberation movements; they seek the freedom to enjoy their basic human rights, maintain their identity and live on their lands. In Canada we are a minority in a nation of twenty-seven million. With a population of fewer than one million, we know we cannot displace the alien government completely, and this is not our objective. The objective is to live together.

But we can at least demand, and we do, the rights that we deserve as First Nations. And these include not only the right to govern ourselves but also the right of our peoples to promote their languages, cultures and traditions and to ensure the integrity of their societies. We have not managed to achieve all that we strive for to improve our situation. These are ongoing battles for future generations. Whatever gains that we have made, they are far from all we need to survive in the future. Other leaders will have to do what they can to promote the rights of our peoples in the next generations.

Will we see real gains on aboriginal and treaty rights in Canada? I am not sure. Governments may back away from their commitments. We do not know where our discussions will lead. We therefore need a strong declaration on indigenous rights in the international arena. But if the gains we make internationally are to be meaningful for us, or other indigenous peoples around the world, they must be implemented in domestic law. We will still have to ensure that the nation-states recognize the rights declared by the United Nations. I caution all those who read this not to indulge the impression that the collective rights of First Nations peoples in Canada are secure. The fact remains that we have only more promises, and we have seen many, many broken promises.

We know from reading the history of our people and witnessing the experiences of other indigenous peoples around the world that we are not alone in suffering the destruction of our lands, cultures, languages and ways of life. I believe that it is of critical importance to end colonialism as it affects all of humanity. Decolonization is a right for all human beings, including the indigenous peoples around the world. We have experienced great pain, immense turmoil in our lives. We have lost our lands, resources and lives. This is part of our shared and common experience as colonized indigenous peoples. We must, as a world community, ensure that we end colonialism. The Beothuk people of what is now called Eastern Canada became victims of European contact. They suffered a genocide and will never walk this earth again. Around the world we know of other examples of original nations, indigenous nations, who have been victims of genocide and we know campaigns of genocide are waged today. Despite what we have suffered as peoples, we denounce violence. We condemn governments that commit acts of genocide against our indigenous brothers and sisters. The First Nations of Canada have awakened to the perils of our brothers and sisters in other parts of the world. The First Nations of Canada are determined to draw attention to governments that have carried out and continue to carry out campaigns of brutality and violence against them. The governments of Indonesia, Peru, Columbia and Guatemala have all exercised active genocide against innocent indigenous peoples, and we grieve for our relatives there. We are very proud of our sister, Rigoberta Menchu, an indigenous woman of Guatemala who was honoured with the Nobel Peace Prize in 1992 for her struggle to liberate her peoples from acts of violence. We applaud her courage and we support her vision of a non-violent society in her country, even as we share her sorrow in not being able to live with her people for fear of government reprisals.

Often we hear the Canadian government make representations about the need for partnership and the importance of creating new relationships with First Nations based on mutual respect. Unfortunately, the truth must be told that we are seldom consulted or involved with our country in developing these statements. They are developed without our input, without partnership. At this point partnership is a goal, not a reality.

There are many things that can be done at the United Nations for indigenous peoples. Mrs. Erica Daes, the Chairwoman of the Working Group on Indigenous Peoples, has proposed the formation of a U.N. Commission on Indigenous Peoples. Under the auspices of the Secretary-General of the United Nations, the mandate of this proposed commission would include the monitoring of human rights violations against indigenous peoples and the support of indigenous peoples around the world.

We urge the United Nations to look at reforms within its own structure to ensure that we have direct participation in decision-making processes. We call upon the governments of the world to meet with us as equals, to respect our peoples as human beings, and to embrace our collective rights. Our common goal must be to end the system of dominance and to replace it with relations based on human rights principles. We must create a new era—a new world—where all people can live in harmony and work together at the international level for the well-being of humankind.

●●●

*In April 1993, the Assembly of First Nations and the National Congress of American Indians jointly sponsored a meeting for the region on indigenous peoples and human rights. The focus of the gathering was to prepare for the United Nations World Conference on Human Rights held in June 1993 in Vienna. The presence of Gaiashkibos, the president of the National Congress of American Indians, served to solidify the relationships between the Chiefs on both sides of the border—a border which is arbitrary for First Nations peoples whose relatives and territories have spanned that geographical line since long before it was imposed. For the Mohawk people from the Akwesasne Reserve, whose territory is in Ontario, Quebec and New York State, border issues are significant; the international border runs right through the Mohawk First Nations. Mohawks travelling from one side of the reserve to the other face customs and tariffs on purchases within their own territories and have complained repeatedly about harassment by customs officers. Other peoples like the Kootenay in British Columbia suffer from the same arbitrary division of their territory by the international border.*

●●●

The peoples of the First Nations want to strengthen relations with our brothers and our sisters in the United States. We are relatives and the international border divides us artificially, breaking up our territories and our families. We did not make this border and we cannot accept it when it separates us from our families. Much more can be done to strengthen our connections and common agendas. We are treaty makers; we have had treaties with other First Nations as well as the Crown. We never surrendered our right to enter into treaties. I think we have to demonstrate this treaty-making history with action—not just words or ambition, but action. So I would like to work towards a treaty between the Assembly of First Nations and the National Congress of American Indians to deal with issues like trade and commerce, economic development, and our culture, language and spirituality as indigenous peoples. The international boundaries were imposed without regard for our territories; they are irrelevant to us, and we can and will ignore them.

There are a number of ways in which we have been deprived of our sovereignty, and one is to have our land and resources taken from us so that we are deprived of the economic capacity to meet the needs of our people. This is how we became dependent on another nation to meet the needs of our people. That has become a path for us of welfare and a path of great grief for our people and we have to reverse that course. We can also, by our own inaction, lose our sovereignty. If we do not respect what self-determination means in terms of how we deal with each other as nations, as distinct peoples, we will deserve to lose our sovereignty. And if we want to protect the rights of our nations, then we must protect and act upon the right of our peoples to enter into treaties with other nations, including other First Nations.

Here in Canada, the treaties that we have with the Crown are not being honoured because the Canadian government wants to forget that we are treaty makers, that it has obligations stemming from its treaty commitments. To honour the treaties would be to continue to recognize the right of our people to make treaties. And who makes treaties? People with self-determination. So long as we are passive, so long as we are apathetic, and so long as we are satisfied with our condition in life today, we ourselves, by our own inaction, will be

responsible for the ultimate defeat of our right of self-
determination, and we will have no one to blame but
ourselves.

Here in Canada, what have we done with our right
of self-determination? I do not ask this to condemn people, but instead to wake people up. Why do we choose
our leaders based on the Indian Act? Why do we not
choose our leaders based on the laws of our own? Why
do we not do it on the basis of our nations? If we do not
take action on self-government, we will always be going
to Parliament, for Parliament to enact laws for our peoples. Some of our Indian leaders are doing this with
respect to our lands: they are asking permission to take
control over their lands. But the land we have is our
land. We should not rely on a White Parliament to tell
us how to govern our lands. That decision rests with our
peoples; it is part of what we call self-determination.
Self-determination is people acting for themselves, not
waiting for another nation to tell them they can move
left or right, backward or forward.

Our peoples across the country are beginning to
face the legacy of their treatment here in Canada.
Whether the issue is residential schools, the justice system or the behaviour of the Department of Indian
Affairs, our people are disclosing the suffering they have
endured, and that is not easy. Our leaders must follow

their lead and begin to disclose the problems they have experienced in the exercise of our right to govern ourselves. Part of what we have to do to achieve this is rid ourselves of layers and layers of skins that we do not need. The snake sheds its skin for new life, but for our people the shedding of just one is not enough. We have so many other skins to get rid of before we can prepare for new life.

Where do the skins that I am referring to come from? They are the skins of colonialism. The skins that convince us we are inferior peoples. The skins that say to our peoples, "Hate yourself because you have been taught to do so and that is your identity." These are the skins that we have to shed. We will not succeed as a people if we continue to rely on another nation to add new identities when our whole effort should be directed at discarding old ones they have already given us.

I know I am not expressing anything that our brothers and sisters in America and around the world have not thought about before. The challenges facing indigenous peoples are common. But I think these challenges need to be stated repeatedly, to be thought about until we can overcome them and end our oppression. We will have to make choices in order to achieve them. We will need to reassess who we are as peoples—not just in Canada, but also in light of our place in the world.

# The Accord That Wasn't

*The debate over the Charlottetown Accord was an intense one for First Nations. In a compressed time-frame, First Nations peoples were asked to participate in intensive negotiations on proposals for constitutional change and to put these proposals to the Chiefs to determine if they were worthy of support. After having been locked out of the Meech Lake round, the opportunity to participate as equals with federal, provincial and territorial governments was a breakthrough for First Nations. The invitation was won only after intense lobbying by Ovide Mercredi and the Chiefs in the months leading up to the negotiations.*

*Constitutional reform has been central to the First Nations agenda for change since the 1970s, when the Trudeau government championed the repatriation of the British North America Act. Because of the recurring nature of Canada's constitutional problems and the need to deal*

with Quebec's grievances, the constitutional reform option
was seen as the strongest strategy for dealing
comprehensively with First Nations issues, especially self-
government. The Assembly of First Nations, along with
Aboriginal leadership from across Canada, went all out on
this front though hopes for reform were subdued after the
four Aboriginal constitutional reform discussions in the
1980s ended in an impasse. When the Charlottetown
Accord round materialized, the leadership was ready to
advocate the changes they wanted, but they were also aware
of how politically unpredictable the process for constitutional
change is in Canada.

The Charlottetown Accord contained the most
comprehensive set of reform proposals on Aboriginal issues
in the history of Canada. The inherent right of self-
government was recognized and Aboriginal governments
were described as one of three orders of government in
Canada. The Accord recognized the need for a treaty review
process and committed the federal government to dealing
with treaty grievances in good faith. The reform package was
sweeping but its real significance stemmed from the fact that
unanimous political agreement was reached on these
heretofore contentious areas. The pressured context of the
Charlottetown round both assisted and troubled First
Nations. On the one hand, there was an opportunity for
significant and rapid political change. On the other, the pace

was too quick to allow Chiefs and First Nations citizens to carefully study the proposals before the Referendum of October 1992.

In the end, the Chiefs were uncomfortable responding to the Charlottetown proposals in the short time available to them between August and October 1992; indeed many received translated versions of the proposals just two weeks before the Referendum. The national debate on the proposals and the prediction of a negative vote by Canadians prevented many of them from stating categorically whether or not they supported the Aboriginal package in the Accord. There was a tacit consensus that individuals or regional organizations could take whatever positions they wanted, but a single national position was not possible without considerable further debate and discussion. Many Chiefs also felt that Canadians should vote on the proposals first to decide if they wanted reconciliation with the First Nations: depending on the result of the first vote, First Nations peoples would vote next. But the Quebec-driven deadline did not offer the luxury of such a process and the comprehensive Referendum went ahead with the now well-known result.

About fifty thousand First Nations people voted on the Accord, a figure that represents only approximately eight percent of the First Nations population. Of the small number of First Nations peoples who did vote, sixty percent rejected the Accord and forty percent supported it. This

*varied by region, with those in the Yukon showing strong
support for the Accord and those in Alberta strongly
rejecting it. Exactly what the First Nations vote means is
difficult, if not impossible, to interpret because of the low
voter turnout and range of items covered by the Accord. It
could mean that the substance of the proposals was rejected.
It could mean the process was rejected. It could mean that
the people who voted against the Accord believed that
something better could be obtained in the future. One thing I
doubt it means is that First Nations peoples are satisfied with
the status quo. Some say the "no" vote by non-Aboriginal
Canadians had little to do with the Aboriginal package, and
that even the "no" side seemed to support the substance and
direction of those proposals. In any case, the Charlottetown
experience was an historic breakthrough: all governments
accepted the inherent right of self-government, agreed to
treaty implementation and accepted Aboriginal peoples as
equal partners in Confederation. From that point there
should be no retreat.*

●●●

In Charlottetown, we gained public support for the
entrenchment of the inherent right of self-government,
not as a delegated form of government but as a pre-existing right of our peoples. You may remember that early in
this struggle the federal and provincial governments

wanted our peoples to define the right before they would
recognize it. We told them we would define it as it
evolves. To pre-define it is to stifle it. We reminded
them that when they created their own governments
here in Canada, they only set out a basic working frame-
work. They have been able to create the society that
they have here today precisely because they had the flexibility to allow for the evolution of their self-government. So it is important for our peoples to have the same
freedom, the same flexibility and opportunity to evolve
forms of government that are acceptable to our peoples.
But to satisfy the non-believers we told them that while
we were not willing to define the right, we were willing
to give it a context and explain its purpose. We told
them that we want our peoples to survive and continue
our distinct ways of life. We do not want to become
assimilated by the dominant society. We have valuable
cultures and precious traditions, and these should prevail
for us, as the original peoples of this territory.

We also persuaded the governments to recognize
that we need a bilateral process, or bilateral processes,
for the implementation of our treaties. This was a very
important gain for all of us. There is currently no political process for any dialogue between First Nations and
the government of Canada on how our treaties should
be implemented by the Canadian government. A

*constitutional* commitment would force the Canadian government to sit down with our peoples, treaty by treaty, to ensure they are implemented, as we understand them. We insisted on a commitment to have an interpretation provision that would make it very clear to the Canadian courts and politicians that our treaties are to be interpreted in a broad, just and liberal manner. This means taking into consideration the spirit and intent of the treaties as we understand them. This is a major gain and one that could lead, ultimately, to the enjoyment of our treaty rights. It would mean that the Canadian government would finally be forced to face up to the fact that the treaties exist, and that the obligations to honour the rights contained in these treaties still hold even though they have chosen to ignore them.

Canadian politicians are afraid of our inherent right of self-government. Some are fearful that it will create legal chaos, which is clearly not true. Some are afraid that it will mean a loss of control over our peoples and our lives. For that reason, many provincial governments are not willing to support the inherent right without a delay in enforcement so they can get used to the idea. They want a transition period. When this issue was being dealt with at the constitutional table, we sought the advice of our leaders. We asked, "Should we agree to a delay of the inherent right of self-government

to allow negotiated agreements with the governments?"
We placed that issue across this country by way of a
faxed letter to all the Chiefs and Councils, all our political organizations. We got a reply, an overwhelming
reply. I was told to accept a delay. Maybe the Chiefs
thought this delay would benefit us, too, by allowing us
to make the transition.

Whatever gains we made in the Charlottetown
process were not made easily. While we may enjoy support from the Canadian people, that does not necessarily mean that we enjoy support from the politicians of
Canada. It was very difficult to get as far as we did. In
many ways it was nothing short of a miracle, considering the enormous resistance to our positions, our rights
and our identity. Everything we gained is fragile. We
have promises and commitments but we have no cer-
tainties. The governments are very careful to say that
everything is subject to approval and review. Nothing is
guaranteed. There is always evidence of people back-
tracking on the commitments and support they gave us
at the table. So the gains that we secured could disappear. We know we could be pushed back down.

*The internal process for developing strategy, discussing
proposals and navigating the rapids is complex and*

challenging for First Nations. There is generally only enough
money available for one representative of each First Nation
to attend a national meeting once each year. For many
participants, gathering in a city like Ottawa involves
journeys of several days.

Then there are the language and cultural differences.
Members of the Assembly of First Nations speak many
different Indian languages and dialects. The majority speak
English as their non-Aboriginal language, but some speak
French but not English. The meetings require expensive,
complicated translation services. Protocol varies depending
upon the traditions and customs of First Nations and Elders
from different regions. For example, some Indian people open
and close a several-day deliberation with a prayer; others pray
each day to open and close meetings. Some First Nations
begin a meeting with a pipe ceremony to honour all of
Creation; others sing their clan song or ask drummers to sing.

The range of concerns that the more than six hundred
bands of the Assembly of First Nations bring to national
meetings makes the process of developing a single national
political strategy complex beyond imagination. At a recent
gathering of Chiefs, the agenda item on self-government
strategies was sidetracked by an Indian Firefighters'
Association resolution and an emergency resolution on the
failure of the federal government to implement the Manitoba
Northern Flood Agreement. It is hard to limit discussions to

*specific areas when the opportunities to gather are so rare and immediate problems cry out for attention. And since most First Nations people face urgent problems at the community level, time spent developing strategy at the national level is a luxury.*

*The fact that First Nations peoples have managed to forge a national movement over the past twenty-five years against all of these odds is a stunning feat of political organization and determination, and an impressive reflection of the will for fundamental change.*

When it comes to First Nations relations with the government of Canada, the recent past has highlighted the strong potential for conflict and confrontation. When people's rights are routinely rejected and denied, they may resort to acts of violence as a means of drawing attention to the problems that need resolution. Violence is contrary to the values and the traditions of the people I represent. Historically, the best efforts on both sides have been to try to find peaceful solutions to troubling problems. For the First Nations, the constitutional changes would have potentially meant the end of dominance, the end of one society ruling over another. The Indian Act has always been the political will of the dominant society, not the political will of the people I represent. It would fall by the wayside with the transition to self-government.

Far too many First Nations, Inuit and Métis people have spent their entire lives in a struggle for their collective rights. It would be far better for our peoples if we were free from that fight. This would allow us to concentrate on rebuilding our economies and governments, strengthening our cultures and healing our people. It would be far better to use our limited energies and resources healing our people than fighting governments to make them acknowledge our rights. The constitutional promise we want to hear is that we can put that fight behind us.

First Nations children in school today do not learn about their place in history. They learn about the place of the settlers. I hope in the future all Canadian children will learn about something called the Aboriginal self-government. Our children should live with a Constitution that explicitly recognizes their peoples' inherent rights to govern themselves. The whole purpose of the provisions in the Charlottetown Accord was to ensure that our peoples can maintain our distinct ways of life, that we are not forced to assimilate. We want our children to learn that being different is not being inferior. When they open their history, social studies, or political science textbooks, we want them to know that they are equals, second to none in Canada.

Pierre Trudeau, a champion of individual rights when he was Prime Minister, came forward during the Charlottetown Accord Referendum debate to criticize the inherent right of self-government and First Nations peoples' collective rights. Let us remember who this Prime Minister is and what role he played in the past. In 1969 his government introduced a White Paper that proposed the end of the Indian Act and the assimilation of our peoples into Canadian society. We saw this as a policy of extermination because it did not propose self-government, it just called for the end of Indian status and Indian rights in Canada. The Assembly of First Nations, through our predecessor organization the National Indian Brotherhood, organized to oppose it. This was an important event for us, not only because it launched our current national organization but also because our reaction to that paper and to the federal government's proposals made it clear that individualism was not our goal. In some ways the White Paper was the First Nations' equivalent of the Lord Durham Report that enraged French-speaking Quebecers. It was a proposal for assimilation into Canada and it showed no recognition or acknowledgment of First Nations treaties or collective rights.

After a great campaign of opposition by great Indian leaders like Harold Cardinal, the Trudeau government withdrew its position and was forced to accept that assimilation was unacceptable. Yet the idea that our people had collective rights was not acceptable to him, either.

During the debate on the Charlottetown Accord proposals, Mr. Trudeau had an opportunity to support our inclusion in the Constitution of Canada, and the recognition of our collective rights. He had a chance to show he had learned something since 1969 about our experiences as First Nations peoples of Canada. We have been trying to educate Canadians about our history, our treaties and our aspirations for better relations. I know Mr. Trudeau is a smart man and I guess I had hoped he would have been listening—that he could see things from our view, too. After his previous mistakes in dealing with our peoples, we hoped he would take advantage of the opportunity to support justice this time around. But what did he do? He attacked the Aboriginal package of the Charlottetown Accord as violating the supremacy of individual rights and potentially establishing governments based on race. His criticisms are unfounded and wrong. It shows me that he sees the world through only his eyes and cannot accept that everyone does not think like he does, that others have different experiences of the world.

First of all, his vision is that our people are just Canadians without special collective rights. According to him, we are like the European newcomers, without any special connection to this place. This is not consistent with our history or with the history of Canada. It is not consistent with our treaties. His vision demands that we conform to Canadian society as individuals and assimilate our cultures and goals with the English and French. He wants us to accept the fact that the system of government that brought us residential schools, the Indian Act and poverty is our salvation. He is seeing the world only from his side. But one must struggle to see it many ways.

Mr. Trudeau's criticisms may seem valid from his vantage point. Canada's individual rights and parliamentary democracy are attractive when one has all the advantages, all the collective and individual benefits of that system. The collective right to the French language and the English language is enshrined in the Constitution. Our language rights are not. His collective right of self-government in the form of Parliament and a legislature is protected in the Constitution. We have no equivalent protection for our government. His government's land and resources are protected in the Constitution. We have no such protection; in fact, our lands and resources have been taken from us.

So I say to Mr. Trudeau, and others who support
his views, it is easy for you to argue the supremacy of
individual rights when you have all the individual rights
and the reason you have them is that because you enjoy
your collective rights, too. This society provides the
security for you to pursue your individual development.
It is not that easy for my people. The peoples I represent
need our collective rights enshrined because we need
the security of sustaining who we are. Individual rights
are important, as I have repeatedly asserted, but you
have to also see that First Nations people have not benefited from your individual rights protections in
Canada. After ten years with your venerated Charter of
Rights and Freedoms we are no better off, Mr. Trudeau.
If individual rights were the panacea for our social and
economic progress, why is it that First Nations peoples
living in cities continue to be discriminated against and
to live in poverty? If individual rights are the solution
for our social and economic progress, why is it that our
people living on reservations are living in poverty? The
fact of the matter is that individual rights alone have
not lifted our people out of the experience of prejudice
and discrimination, and they cannot.

You have argued that our governments are based
on race and the Charlottetown Accord would therefore
entrench racially based governments. This is untrue.

We need protection for our identity, language and culture. This is not racism—it is cultural preservation. Our communities are not, nor would they ever be, closed to non-Indian people. We simply want to have the authority to promote and protect our identities and the only way we can do this is by having some control over our lives. You would be welcome to become part of one of our communities, Mr. Trudeau, but we would expect you to respect our beliefs, to learn our language and to accept the authority and jurisdiction of our First Nations governments.

How else can we protect our identities? If we become Canadians who vote every few years for a government, we would be destroyed. We do not have the numbers to have a meaningful voice in the electoral system. That system is all about numbers and majorities and it is not designed to accommodate our peoples. Either we find an alternative or we are assimilated. In 1969, we made it clear to your government that we will not accept assimilation and we maintain that position today.

●●●

*The rejection of the Charlottetown Accord was a disappointment to all four of the national Aboriginal leaders who negotiated it, campaigned for it, and sought to improve*

*the conditions of Aboriginal peoples in Canada. The
disappointment stemmed from the realization that after all
the resources and effort in developing and designing new
approaches and strategies for reconciliation, in the span of
one day the whole package could be dropped. And so it was
when then Prime Minister Brian Mulroney announced that
the Charlottetown Accord was dead with the "no" result.
First Nations leaders knew only too well that few politicians
would touch Aboriginal rights issues after the bitter sting of a
defeated referendum. This is what has happened since
October 1992. The great support that was shown for
Aboriginal and treaty rights by the public and governments
has led nowhere after the Referendum result. Where it will
lead from here is uncertain.*

* * *

The demise of the Charlottetown Accord in October
1992 transformed the First Nations agenda for change
in Canada. People have reassured me since then that
there is support for the inherent right of self-government, despite the rejection of the Accord, but I do not
really see it. No doubt there is general political support
from the public. In practical terms, however, there will
be no progress on the right of self-government until positive changes in national policies and laws are made.
This takes more than public support. It takes political

change. If the law does not explicitly recognize our inherent right of self-government, and our peoples try to assert it, as they will do, they will be told by govern-ments and bureaucrats that they have no existing rights. Positive public sentiment is nice, but we need actual changes in the legal and political structure of this country.

In practical terms, we are back to where we were before the Charlottetown Accord was negotiated. We must now look outside the constitutional reform agenda for new vehicles for change. Whatever opinions you may have had, whether you were for or against the Accord, it outlined a process that would have resulted in the orderly implementation, over a period of years, of the right of our peoples to govern themselves. It would have made it possible for First Nations peoples to begin to peacefully implement our forms of government, whether on a community, regional or national basis, according to our own values and priorities. It would not have been easy, but it would have been possible.

So what are our options now? This is what I ask the Canadian people. What options have you given us? The only option I see is for my peoples to assert the right to govern ourselves unilaterally, whether the law recognizes it or not. How long can we wait for change? Constitutional change has been a disappointment to us again. Will the next federal government return to the table? Will it be inclined to carry on comprehensive discussions for constitutional reform with our people? These are the questions and the consequences for First Nations. It is not as easy as just taking the Charlottetown Accord's proposals on self-government and putting them in place without the other parts of that Accord. The Referendum has been interpreted by the politicians as a "no" to everything, including our peoples' rights.

Who will form the next government? What will its positions be on our issues? Where does the new leader stand? The personalities in federal politics are changing. Those whom we've educated about our situation are leaving politics. We will have to start again. What process will be available to carry on this dialogue with Canada? Will it remedy the injustices of the people I represent? Will there be social peace between Canada and the First Nations, or will there be more confrontation? I do not know the answers to those questions. We have to ask the political parties what their positions are on our issues. How do they propose to deal with the unfinished First Nations agenda? We want a process that would not result in confrontation, that would not mean barricades. What are their ideas? We must closely examine their approaches and answers.

What do the people I represent do now? Do we wait for several years, and allow the status quo to prevail? What would that mean for the status of our rights? Can we afford to wait while our rights are trampled, or must we do something to assert those rights now, in order to protect them for future enjoyment by our peoples? How much more can our people suffer? These are not rhetorical questions; they are practical and pressing. For example, in the provinces of Manitoba and Saskatchewan, reserves are developing gaming establishments to create employment and wealth for their people. Some bands are tired of government intransigence and they are just going ahead and doing it. This has meant confrontations, raids, and rising hostilities. Without a process to talk things through and find solutions, we will have conflict.

First Nations see gaming as a part of our inherent right of self-government, as part of our jurisdiction and our economic future. If there is no way to negotiate self-government, we will just do it. We will not accept that only two levels of government, the federal and provincial governments, can exercise jurisdiction over gaming. The people I represent see many non-Aboriginal governments setting up gaming institutions in restaurants and the province of Manitoba creating its own casino. Everybody else seems to be taking the opportunity to raise revenue for public services, but our people are told, "No, you cannot do likewise."

First Nations peoples are not inclined to wait for our rights to be recognized in light of this double standard. Bands are going ahead and asserting their jurisdiction over gaming, and finding investors to help them set up operations. This is happening not only in the province of Manitoba but in New Brunswick, too. It is going to happen in Ontario and across the country. So for the next two years, Canadians and their governments and Aboriginal leaders are going to be faced with the reality of de facto self-government, in which our people will simply assert their jurisdiction. They will do it without discussion and they will not wait for permission from the federal or provincial governments. What will happen when they assert their power? Our experience in Canada shows us that when people take power, it usually means a confrontation.

Is direct action the only strategy our peoples have available? What are the alternatives? We made these agreements in our treaties with Canada in good faith. We have satisfied our side of the bargain, but the government has not satisfied its side. It takes the benefits readily but forgets its obligations. We will not sit by and see our peoples and resources exploited.

So there are problems with waiting for a better day.

We cannot afford to bide our time. If we wait for the inherent right of self-government to be recognized in the Constitution at some uncertain future point, or if we wait for the courts to define it, what will we have left when they get around to it? And we do not have a say in the courts. We are not part of the Supreme Court of Canada. When the courts look at the inherent right, they will see it only through their eyes and training. They do not know our history and our peoples and they do not even know much about our rights. We cannot afford the expense of court battles against a highly powerful government. So why should we look forward to a court process when our experiences over the past 125 years lead us to predict, with some certainty, that it will result in a one-sided vision?

For the sake of social peace in Canada, we have to find some new political pathways in the wake of Charlottetown. We need a political process to resolve the disputes that have been there for a long, long time or we will face confrontations and blockades, or continual run-ins with the RCMP.

What are the alternatives? I repeat myself because I am genuinely asking the question and I do not know the answer. I need ideas, opinions and direction—not just from the people I represent, although I am gathering their direction and their insight, but from other

Canadians as well. Your opinions on how to change this political situation are important and will help shape the next government's position on treaty and aboriginal rights in Canada.

Our peoples will assert our rights; it is just a question of how we direct our energy. We must be careful as a country because if we adopt an approach other than kindness, we will go down the path of violence. This is a real issue and one I worry about. The leadership I want to provide in the Assembly of First Nations is one of social peace, and this is the message I want to send to the rest of Canada as well. But the support of Canadians is needed for me to be able to take this position because my people cannot continue to be left out in the cold. If the government backs away from accepting our rights, there will be confrontations. Canada has an obligation, just as we do, to maintain social peace. But things can go very wrong. We saw that happen not too long ago. We do not want to repeat the cycle of denial of rights and confrontation.

# Paddling More Peaceful Rivers

The situation for First Nations people in Canada is, as the Canadian Human Rights Commission suggested a few years ago, a national disgrace. The social costs are inestimable because the contributions First Nations peoples can make to Canadian society are being thwarted. And the financial cost of ongoing confrontation is enormous. Canada's reputation as a world leader in the protection and promotion of human rights is far from secure in light of the treatment of Aboriginal peoples. Yet Canada's role could be reversed and genuine leadership could be demonstrated if the deplorable state of human rights protection for First Nations individuals and communities was finally addressed. The magnitude of the tragedy can seem overwhelming, but it is not without solutions.

The status quo continues for one very simple reason—because there is a lack of political commitment to change the situation. Outside of the Charlottetown Accord experience, which was in many ways a breakthrough and hopefully not an anomaly, governments have not worked cooperatively towards change. Canadian governments have always adopted adversarial opening positions towards the recognition of aboriginal and treaty rights. We must struggle against this. For example, when the federal government comes to negotiate land claims with First Nations, a typical starting premise is that the particular First Nation actually has no legally enforceable rights. This stance makes the process appear like a demonstration of the magnanimity of the government and turns the whole debate into an elaborate charade with First Nations representatives forced to beg in order to achieve any gains. And when the begging is addressed to low-level bureaucrats without the power to make decisions, we have to perform the humiliating charade over and over again. This is why First Nations frustrations build.

It has taken civil disobedience, armed confrontation, suicides and other dramatic events for First Nations peoples to garner some commitment from government to make meaningful changes. First Nations are left with few options at the moment, short of confrontation, because there are no functioning or established political forums to address First Nations questions. Despite the hard work of individual Aboriginal politicians like Ethel Blondin and Willy Littlechild, our peoples' views and approaches are not effectively represented in Parliament or the legislative assemblies of the provinces where representation is based on size of population and party organization. The mainstream political system is not workable for First Nations, not only because it fails to recognize the special place of Aboriginal peoples as other than ordinary Canadian voters, but also because it does not fully accord with First Nations political traditions and practices. More creative political arrangements are required.

First Nations people, with a population of only approximately three-quarters of one million to one million people dispersed across the nation, are never going to be well represented within the traditional Canadian political system. And First Nations peoples are not likely to vote or get involved extensively in the political party system because there are more fundamental grievances with the political system that need to be addressed, like the fact that these representative bodies have done so much to attempt to assimilate First Nations through techniques like the Indian Act. Hence confrontation, and in some cases armed confrontation, has been a method for garnering political attention and extracting commitments to solving First Nations problems. Clearly, this is not a basis upon which to build a durable cooperative relationship between First Nations and Canadians. It reflects a breakdown in the relationship and even if it sometimes leads to a breakthrough, it comes with a cost. Confrontation breeds suspicion, an aggressive police presence and potentially the loss of life.

We have to find a better path for addressing the situations of First Nations in Canada. There are concrete options. One would expect that the advances accepted in principle in the Charlottetown Accord, such as the inherent right of self-government, have made the political climate for change in Canada more favourable than in the past. Unfortunately, little momentum has been shown politically for change since those discussions fell apart in October 1992. But the problems endure. One encouraging aspect of the Charlottetown Accord Referendum result was that despite the negative vote, the public support for the Aboriginal component was significant and strong. While that may be somewhat reassuring, it is also true that public support without the commitment of politicians to act provides little solace or hope for those in desperate need. Public support alone will not change our situation. We need political action at the highest levels and we need it urgently. The group suicide attempt by the children in Davis Inlet in early 1993 was a cry of desperation we cannot erase or ignore. It called out for response, urgent action. The impetus for change must be faced and the responsibility is squarely on the shoulders of governments, especially the federal government in light of its historic and special relationship with First Nations.

Of course, key sectors in Canadian society like labour and business must and do push for change to encourage solutions to the problems we are experiencing, but the current governments will be the ones charged with making the first critical steps for change. In some parts of Canada, provincial governments are establishing creative forums like the British Columbia Treaty Commission to accommodate discussions on many issues, such as those raised in this book. These signs are heartening but they require national coordination and the participation and leadership of the federal government. The federal government needs to take the first significant step since Charlottetown and make a commitment to the resolution of First Nations disputes in a manner consistent with the aboriginal and treaty rights of First Nations and with its duties as a fiduciary or trustee for the interests of First Nations. To make the government's job clearer, we've presented in the following pages six specific ideas for change that we believe are worthy of immediate discussion and action.

**Inherent Right of Self-Government**: The federal government should not delay in moving away from the Indian Act and towards joint implementation of the inherent right of self-government. They should immediately introduce in Parliament a declaration recognizing the inherent right of self-government as part of the existing constitutional law of Canada, reinforced by the treaties. This declaration could describe a process, previously agreed upon by First Nations, for the gradual transition away from the Indian Act and into new arrangements with First Nations emphasizing self-government and the exercise of jurisdiction by First Nations over our people and territories. Those First Nations prepared to start discussing their government's areas of jurisdiction—such as child welfare, education, economic development and justice—would meet with senior federal and provincial political representatives (not only bureaucrats) to formalize new relationships among the governments and First Nations. These new relationships may take the form of new treaties or agreements to implement existing treaties.

**Treaties:** The federal government, as the Crown's representative in the treaties, should begin a process of implementation discussions with any First Nation that wishes to have its treaty honoured. This process, which could be part of or separate from the self-government discussions, must consider the First Nations views of the treaties and be open to reviewing the fraud, misrepresentation and abuse that government officials inflicted upon First Nations at treaty time. Where treaty promises that certain lands will be set aside for First Nations remain unfulfilled, priority should be given to correcting these breaches and compensating First Nations for the failure to deliver on the Crown's explicit promises of continued autonomy and economic well-being.

The treaty process must respect the way treaties were entered into by the First Nations and the Crown, acknowledging the equality of the parties and the role of First Nations customs and traditions in solemnizing their affairs through agreements. It would be appropriate for the federal government to appoint treaty commissioners for each treaty area to conduct or oversee these discussions. The treaty commissioners would require independence from government to ensure that they can honestly address the implementation of treaties without engaging in party politics and without adopting adversarial approaches to First Nations peoples. They would

have to work with provincial governments to ensure
that the commitments in the treaties are honoured by
provincial governments as well.

**Culture, Language and Spirituality**: A significant commitment is needed to keep First Nations languages alive
and vibrant for future generations. Languages that are
nearly lost need urgent action for regeneration. Of the
fifty-three aboriginal languages in Canada, only three
have a fighting chance of surviving into the next century with a sufficient number of proficient speakers to sustain them unless immediate measures are taken. This is
the legacy of residential schools where First Nations
peoples were punished for speaking their languages. It is
also the legacy of neglect and the belief in the inferior
status of First Nations peoples, languages and cultures.
Urgent action is required to increase aboriginal language instruction in schools in First Nations communities as well as in public schools, and to extend this
instruction to adults where communities desire it.
Emphasis on bilingual and bicultural education in
English or French and First Nations languages should
be the priority in First Nations education. Even off-
reserve there should be programs to ensure that where
there are sufficient numbers of First Nations students,
there will be aboriginal language instruction geared

towards proficiency in Canadian schools. The teachers
in these programs should not, in all cases, require formal
education; preference must be given to those who are
knowledgeable about the languages.

It follows that First Nations languages should be
the official languages for First Nations communities
and greater translation and communications services
should be available for First Nations people whose first
language is neither English nor French. These language protections are inextricably linked to the revitalization of First Nations culture and spirituality and
to the larger reconciliation which needs to take place
between the First Nations and Canada. There should
be federal legislation guaranteeing, in the most generous and appropriate way, the greatest possible cultural
and spiritual freedom for First Nations. This would
include the right to have access to, if not control over,
sacred sites, and the right to practise one's culture and
spirituality freely throughout the country including
within prisons. This kind of legislation is both symbolic and politically potent. First Nations have experienced the near-total destruction of our culture and
spirituality through our encounter with the Canadian
church and state. This is not to say that the church has
not become, in many important respects, integrated
into First Nations culture and spirituality, but it has

certainly not replaced First Nations culture and spirituality, and we need a clear demonstration of respect for First Nations cultures.

The protection of First Nations culture and spirituality must also involve the restitution and return of sacred and important cultural objects taken from First Nations individuals and communities through theft and by both unscrupulous and well-intentioned art and museum dealers and officials. A joint federal-First Nations office should be established to help First Nations locate sacred objects like medicine bundles, drums and rattles and return them to their communities. The government and the museums must acknowledge the continuing and vibrant nature of First Nations culture and discard the notion that it is vanishing and can therefore be relegated to the dustbins of history.

Beyond this, there should be much more extensive and contemporary-focused education about First Nations for non-Aboriginal peoples in Canadian schools. This education should be oriented towards building respectful and sustaining relations for the future and replacing racially offensive and culturally inappropriate materials with those prepared in consultation with First Nations peoples. This education initiative should also include teaching new immigrants as well as citizens about our rights and perspectives.

**Lands, Resources and Environment**: The federal gov-ernment policy on land claims needs to be abandoned and a just, fair and principled policy in the form of legis-lation needs to be put in its place. This new policy should be the product of discussions between First Nations leaders and government—it should be endorsed by both parties. It should be premised on a recognition of First Nations land rights. There are ongoing con-frontations throughout the country over lands and resources and it should be a government priority to pre-vent them. The new policy should require an indepen-dent body to assess, negotiate and resolve land claims, with equal representation on such a body by govern-ment and First Nations representatives. Strict time-frames should be adopted for each claim to ensure they are settled in a timely fashion. A land claims court should be established to deal with conflicts in the nego-tiation and policy implementation process and to devel-op expertise on legal questions relating to land claims so that these conflicts can be kept out of Canadian courts where they take too much time and money and inevitably lead to unsatisfactory results.

Major development projects should not proceed without the agreement of First Nations peoples in the territory affected, particularly in the Canadian North. Special consideration should be given to the impact of any development project on First Nations peoples and lifestyles, and decisions to proceed with development should be reached only with the free consent of the First Nations affected.

**Health**: There is an urgent need for a First Nations crisis intervention team to address the dire situation facing First Nations youth in many communities across the country. Such a crisis intervention team should be co-ordinated nationally by First Nations communities and would need to involve Elders, social workers, counsellors, and alcohol and drug therapists. It would be the goal of the crisis intervention team to support communities, when requested, in their efforts to respond to the problems which First Nations youth and adults are experiencing. It should be geared towards healing and achieve this by helping the community restore the balance in their relationships with each other instead of by taking individuals with problems away from community intervention. Urgent action is required to address health problems related to poverty.

**Fiscal and Economic Arrangements**: The poverty in First Nations communities has to be seriously tackled by the federal, provincial and First Nations governments. First Nations need to participate in the regular First

Ministers conferences on the economy in order to end First Nations poverty. Greater First Nations control over efforts to attract investment and develop sustainable community economic development projects is desperately required. The progressively declining levels of funding to First Nations in all sectors has to be reversed because First Nations communities alone cannot shoulder the urgent need for assistance. Priority should be given to ensuring that the basic infrastructure such as water, sewage and roads is present and functioning in all First Nations communities without delay or exception.

Poverty will be overcome in partnership with the business community and through the elimination or relaxing of government regulation of sustenance activities like hunting, trapping and fishing. Preferential taxation laws to attract business and community-owned and regulated gaming facilities are two initiatives that need closer consideration. The welfare cycle in First Nations communities needs to be broken, and it will only happen through clear planning and the development of a national anti-poverty strategy for First Nations. So much of our peoples' health and well-being is connected to eradicating poverty that in order to enable First Nations to make a vibrant contribution to Canada we need to deal with that poverty.

Each component of the six-part agenda outlined above represents past failure and present opportunity. The goal in all the initiatives we've described here is to correct the national tragedy we face and to do so through healing First Nations and healing Canada. The legacy of discrimination, domination and disrespect for the rights of First Nations has not left an attractive impression of Canada and has become a leitmotif of Canadian history. While none of us knows exactly what the future holds, we do know that Canadians and First Nations are in these rapids together and that navigating the turmoil we collectively face will require skill and commitment. By ignoring the situation we invite greater social unrest and certain confrontation. In endeavouring to build bridges where there are conflicts we will find the calmer waters, which will make our voyage together on this part of Turtle Island an adventure instead of a calamity. The dream is for a better Canada for everyone and a better five hundred years ahead for First Nations.

As we write, the long awaited Royal Commission on Aboriginal Peoples is well into its mandate. First Nations applaud the goodwill and resolve the Commission indicates. However, we have learned not to put all of our cargo in one canoe. The Government of Canada should act now on the issues we have outlined while anticipating the final report of the Royal

Commission which will be much broader and more detailed than our suggestions here.

Canada's former Chief Justice Brian Dickson believes that the Royal Commission on Aboriginal Peoples, which is due to report in late 1994 or early 1995, has the potential to be an important instrument for education and reconciliation in Canada. The Royal Commission was appointed in 1991 with a large mandate to propose recommendations for the future relationship between Aboriginal peoples and Canada. In a 1991 letter to the Prime Minister, Brian Dickson said that "the vast majority of Canadian Natives—and I mean ordinary Native people, not just their political leaders—are deeply frustrated and profoundly disappointed with the way they perceive that they have been and are today treated by Canadian governments of all levels, and with their current economic, social and cultural positions in the system."

While it may sometimes seem that we are entering a new phase of reconciliation because of progress we are making in bringing our issues forward, this deep sense of frustration is present today at the same level, with the same intensity, as it was when former Chief Justice Dickson was prompted to write those words. We are frustrated. We are disappointed with Canada, with our

treatment by governments and by the people of Canada.
We welcome attempts to change this situation and to
give us hope.

There is not a single First Nations person in
Canada who has not been a victim of power—not just
the abuse of it but the lack of it. You see, we have experienced it both ways. We have little power of our own,
and yet we suffer the abuse of those who enjoy it.
When the Royal Commission sees evidence of dominance and the abuse of power, whether in our communities or within the Canadian governments, it is the
duty of its members to expose it. We need their recommendations for solutions to the problems that face us
all in Canada. But the goodwill that exists for change is
beginning to disappear on our side. First Nations peoples are hardening in our views. We are frustrated.
There has to be an end to paternalism, a quick end to
our treatment as inferiors, or the chances for solutions
will begin to evaporate.

The solutions to these many problems can begin to
be found by adopting the perspective of the Aboriginal
peoples. People need to see it our way for a change, to
accept us, our ways of life, our world views. They need
to accept a basic principle we all grew up with: that of
respect for the right to be different, of respect for co-
existence. We hope those who work for the

Commission will think of it in this way, that they will take our view and work towards respect.

We would prefer to have a more positive message, a lighter approach. But we are affected, all of us, by this history of being victims. We sometimes react as a victim does, with anger. We have to guard against that too. We feel the anger of being mistreated and struggle to turn that into kindness even towards those who are unkind to our people. It is not easy, and if our situation is not addressed it will become even harder.

Let us share our dream for First Nations peoples. It is a dream about the collective rights most Canadians take for granted—about rights and responsibilities we cherish for ourselves. We dream about a Canada in which our inherent right to govern ourselves is acknowledged. About a time when we can use our own political judgment, our own free will to shape our destinies and control our own affairs. We dream about healthy communities where children will be proud to say they are First Nations peoples. You see, this is what self-government or self-determination is about for our peoples. It is about self-respect, self-esteem and the future of our distinct cultures and identities. Self-determination is a basic human right. It is enshrined in international laws, discussed in religious scriptures and extolled in music and literature. Yet we have been denied that right. Or, more accurately, it has been kept from us despite many signed treaties and well-intentioned promises that our identities and our rights as distinct peoples would be protected and acknowledged.

Our peoples dream about the survival of our languages and cultures. We want to be able to ensure that our children are taught our languages in schools, that they in fact attend our own institutions of education. We dream about a future in which we will not be placed in the position of having to beg the rest of Canada for the land that once belonged to our ancestors, land we still use. We seek a place within Canada for the jurisdiction of our governments, for our political will—a place where we can find full expression of our self-determination without breaking up this viable young nation-state. We are seeking a place where we can make decisions about how we will share the natural resources available to us in a way that is consistent with our own view of the Earth, our own economic agendas and our own values with respect to development that does not destroy the land.

Above all, our dream is for equality as peoples and for the respect of our right to be different. We want a new balance in our relationships within Canada. We do not wish to continue to face an imposed vision of who we should be, and of how we should conduct our affairs.

Canadians often ask, "Why is self-government important? What will it accomplish in the real world?" Self-government is about an end to dominance of one group of people over another. It means that, for the first time in our history, our peoples will have the freedom of choice that is the essence of self-determination. For example, it provides the right and the responsibility to choose a child welfare system that meets our needs. Self-government offers the ability to develop classroom programs that breed hope and create real opportunities for our youth. It offers us the tools of economic development, income and the ability to begin healing from within and to combat social ills like child abuse and alcoholism. Self-government will accomplish much in the real world. The exact path of the future no one knows, but this is a correct direction.

Our faith in self-government is not that it will be a panacea. On its own, self-government will not correct past injustices. Nor will it, in itself, reduce the burden of poverty or remove all the barriers to a better future. It is a beginning; not a solution. The fears people have about self-government result from a lack of trust and willingness to embrace change. The recognition of our inherent right to govern ourselves does not mean that Canada will be dismembered. It does not mean that our people will create their own military organizations. It does not mean that we will be rushing off to write our own criminal codes or rejecting all federal and provincial laws and creating chaos. We believe that many Canadians share and support our dream of a better future. They want historic progress to address the many problems that our people face. We are grateful for that support and we are encouraged by it.

But throughout history there have been many broken promises. We do not put too much faith in new promises because we have learned not to expect too much. There have simply been too many shattered dreams. Broken promises break trust. Broken promises break nations. First Nations cannot accept more broken or empty promises. We do not believe Canadians want that approach either. Canadians can help us enjoy our basic human rights by informing the politicians that they share the dream of a better future for all of us, by asking them to negotiate with us in good faith on the problems we have, by reminding them that they hold the power to break the pattern of broken promises. They have the power to make history, and to uphold the honour of Canada for all of us.

Ovide Mercredi
Mary Ellen Turpel
Ottawa, Ontario
June 1993